T0283574

Jo McCarroll's

Vege Patch
from scratch

Jo McCarroll's

Vege Patch
from scratch

upstart press

Contents

This is my garden in the Auckland suburbs.

Harvest recipes

I threw a few of my favourite recipes in too: ones I cook myself a lot, or have had shared with me by friends and family. Well, I say recipes, apart from the preserves, which I make exactly as described, the rest are more like meal inspiration, and flexible enough that you can sub ingredients in and out depending on what you have growing. I like to harvest first and then cook a meal based on what I have lots of, rather than have a recipe that needs to be followed exactly and start by making a list of what I am out of! I hope there's something there that becomes a favourite for you.

Bottom four pics, clockwise from top left: Me and a 'Rampicante' zucchini; homegrown preserves; gherkins pre-pickling; an eggplant.

Introduction

The reason I started gardening was to grow food. I was, and still am, a very keen cook and preserver. This was a long time ago, and there were lots of vegetables and herbs that I would read about in international cookbooks that you just couldn't buy easily, if at all, in New Zealand. I thought I might as well try and grow a few things myself. And so I did.

And indeed I still do. I love growing vegetables and herbs and produce a heap of fresh food from my Auckland backyard. Not just to save money, although it does help keep food bills down, especially now with vege prices what they are. But also, frankly, it's a nice way to live. I like having fresh veges immediately on hand. I like cooking and eating organically and seasonally. I like throwing fresh herbs into whatever I make with abandon. I love serving salad so fresh it's photosynthesising. And when it's time to make dinner, I'd rather wander round the garden than the supermarket.

It just makes sense to grow a bit yourself to be honest. Sometime I am a little surprised more people don't do it. It doesn't have to take much time, cost much or require much space. And it's not that it's easy, exactly, but there's ways to make vege gardening easier and more productive. And there's stuff that, once you understand it, will help set you up for success.

So I hope there's something in these pages that inspires you to get growing. I don't care what takes your fancy, whatever you plant or sow, I hope it flourishes for you. And I hope growing your own fresh food brings a lot of fun and satisfaction to your life. I know it does to mine.

Jo

Jo McCarroll

My untidy garden in
Auckland's Mt Albert.

How to get growing

If you want to set your vegetable garden up for success: get the site right, the scale right, the timing right and the plants right.

There is some basic stuff worth knowing, which will help you grow pretty much everything.

One of the reasons I have never tried to write a vegetable gardening book before is they can be so repetitive. Sometimes it feels like they all say the same things. Every plant needs sun, every plant needs water, almost every plant appreciates fertile soil and good drainage.

The thing is those things are true and bear repeating. But that's the other issue I have with gardening advice in general. I find it tends to fall into two camps: either growing veges is made to sound absurdly simplistic – just remember to water the garden and you will quickly and easily be self-sufficient (you won't). Or it's made to sound really, really complicated, like you need an advanced qualification in soil science and outdoor crop production just to begin (you don't).

I think growing vegetables is fun. It's good for you both mentally and physically. It's not that it's easy, exactly, more it's surprisingly easy to grow some stuff, and there's a lot you can do to make it easier and more likely to be successful. It doesn't have to take much work, or take up much of your time or need much space. And sometimes things go wrong, but if you understand a few fundamental things you can start to see what things went wrong and make some adjustments. That way, every time something goes wrong, you learn from it.

It's often said that the best way to learn how to grow something is to fail at growing it. I have certainly learned a lot more over the years from my failures than from my successes.

People sometimes say to me they'd like to grow vegetables but they tried once and failed. I think that's sad. Gardening isn't a test you can fail. You always get another go.

What's the worst that can happen? Say, your plants die. I mean that's a bummer of course, try and work out what went wrong, so you can change it up next time to grow the same thing. But apart from that just don't worry too much. Most of what I have learned about gardening is from trial and error: error is part of it. I don't know any gardener who won't admit to killing a few plants over the years. I have killed loads of them myself and I literally write about growing them for a living. The police never come. It's honestly fine to just bury any victims in your garden in this instance: it all helps build up soil fertility.

All gardeners start somewhere. So start where you are. If you are new to gardening, start small. Focus on what grows well for you and where you live. React to what you see and feel rather than sticking to a schedule. Don't be afraid to get your hands dirty. Celebrate your wins and learn from your losses. And that's what gardening success looks like to me.

An early autumn harvest.

Sun, shelter and site

Edible plants need sunlight to grow. Some can manage with a bit less of it, sure: lettuces and leafy greens, say, appreciate some afternoon shade at the height of summer. But you can create shade, it's fast and easy to do. You can even, to an extent, create or at least amplify the available heat. But you cannot create light. The best spot for your vegetable garden is the very sunniest spot on your property and the colder your climate the more important it is that you set up your growing space somewhere that gets sunlight throughout the day.

Permaculture garden design starts with what is called a base map, where you make a scale drawing of the property and add all the elements you have and wish to keep (such as your house, the driveway, fences, any existing trees). Then you can layer onto the map (or a copy of it) where the shadows fall in different seasons, what the soil is like in different parts of the garden, where the wind comes from, and any particularly pernicious weeds you want to avoid. You can even future-proof by planning for how big you expect certain trees to get. It's actually a sensible thing to do whether you are a permaculturist or not.

But even if you don't want to make a site map, spend time getting to know your site before you do anything permanent, like building raised beds or planting trees.

In particular, it's useful to know where the sun falls over the year. You want to know where the shadows are and how they fall over the whole day. Try checking and recording at mid-morning, noon and mid-afternoon on the winter solstice and on the summer solstice. There is a whole host of apps online you can use that show the sun's movement, sunlight phases and predict the size of shadow on any given day and a certain location, or just do it in real life by looking at the real shadows on the solstices (or any day within a few weeks of the solstices, it doesn't have to be exact).

Sunlight is the most important factor by a country mile, but shelter is important too. You want good airflow for plant health but avoid windy or exposed spots if you can. Edible crops don't like wind at all, even if it doesn't blow

How to make a base map. I made one for my place just by putting my address into Google maps, zooming in on my boundaries, printing the image and then tracing it. If you do that, remember to copy the scale bar from Google maps too as it will help when you keep any elements you add to scale.

them right over (and it doesn't take much to topple top-heavy tall crops such as corn and tomatoes) it stresses them out. Bees and other pollinators don't like wind, plus it wicks moisture from the soil like nobody's business, which will make the garden a lot more work for you. If you are on a coastal property, or you are trying to grow vegetables on an apartment balcony, it can be very hard to avoid the wind: so create porous wind shelters with hedges or trellis if you can, or rig up temporary ones with windbreak cloth. And if all else fails focus on lower-growing edible crops, which will cope better.

In kitchen design, there's a theory known as the golden triangle which arranges the three main work areas (the sink, the fridge and the hob) in a loose triangle so you can move easily from one to the other without bottlenecks, backtracking or wasted steps. I think you can apply that to vegetable garden design actually – site your garden within easy access of what you will need to maintain it. In particular the taps (nothing will quell your enthusiasm for homegrown vegetables faster than carting water any distance) and wherever you store your tools and gear. I would site your vegetable-growing area so it's easy to get to from the house too, particularly from the kitchen. If you are putting in pathways make sure they are wide enough for a loaded wheelbarrow and if you are setting up beds, don't make them too big: you want to be able to reach easily into the middle from the side (my beds are 1.5m square, which is the limit of my arm's reach).

Now some of this is bleeding obvious and some isn't, at least it wasn't to me. My house is brick and the walls form natural heat sinks, absorbing warmth from the sun during the day and releasing it at night. I only realised that after I had lived here a couple of years by which stage I'd planted a passionfruit in one place when another spot would have been considerably better. One of my raised beds is partly in a rain shadow from my shed, another is getting increasingly shaded out by a plum tree that keeps growing bigger. My beds run roughly from north to south; east to west would have been a better choice in terms of access to light (however your vegetable rows should run north to south to get the maximum benefit from sunlight). There's an old aphorism that an hour of planning can save you 10 hours of doing: this is very true in gardening. Frankly, I would have been better to put more time into planning than I did.

But at the same time, I know for me, in the beginning, it felt a little overwhelming trying to triangulate the contours of the landscape to anticipate all the potential intersections and changes that the future might bring. So don't get paralysed trying to find the absolutely perfect spot. There isn't one, honestly, you always need to compromise on some aspect. If you want a garden, start one. Bung some seeds in or plant something in a pot or container, what do you have to lose? You can move it around while you get to know the lay of the land. Just keep it manageable and fun. If gardening starts to feel like homework you are doing it wrong.

Keep a garden diary. Even just recording dates you sow or plant is worthwhile. A friend uses a photo album, she writes the date she plants on the plant label and pops it in a plastic pocket.

It is easy to create shade. This is Diana Maunder's Kāpiti Coast garden. She puts up cheap beach umbrellas in summer over the hottest part of the day, and they work well, she says, she doesn't have to water as often and is able to go away for a few days and not return to dying plants.

Starting small
is still starting

Look, if you are new to gardening or you have tried and failed before, then start small. You don't need to plant every crop you might want to grow in the first year, in fact I strongly suggest you don't. I was talking to Carl Freeman the other day, a former New Plymouth market gardener who now teaches horticulture at the Western Institute of Technology at Taranaki Te Pūkenga, and he said he'd recently met someone who had planted 100 tomatoes. "And I just knew, if he was growing that many, they were going to be neglected," he told me. "And more likely to have disease and problems. So he'll get a low harvest for the effort he is putting in. Whereas I have six 'Moneymaker' tomatoes in my garden. They are growing in really good soil, they are growing up a trellis, they are very well cared for. And I am getting so many tomatoes off each plant. The freezer is packed with tomatoes, we have made lots of sauces, and we have been eating tomatoes every day. One of my first mentors used to say that growing fewer plants better is better than growing lots of plants not as well."

This is a hard lesson for me and one I am still learning. I love sowing seeds. It's fun trying new vegetable varieties. I am a chronic over-planter. But there is honestly no point planting more than you have space to grow. Even if you have the space, there's no point planting more than you will maintain, or more than you can eat, preserve or give away; you end up putting time and energy into crops that only feed the compost. Not that having more plants means you increase your yield either – as Carl says, one very well-maintained tomato can produce a huge amount of fruit, and quite likely more than several that are just limping along. That's true of other crops too. This is worth remembering if you are an experienced gardener, as I said, I need reminding of it myself. But it's especially true if you are starting out. The key thing that keeps a new gardener interested is an early success, so only plant what you can maintain so you can lavish your time and attention on what you grow.

Before you buy any plant ask yourself two questions. Do I have room for this? And will it thrive in the conditions offered in my garden? Do not wander around a garden centre buying what looks good that day and then get home and work out where to fit it in. I mean, I do that too sometimes, I have to admit. But planning then planting is a better order.

A salad planter at my back door. Leafy greens are a great crop to grow at home. I read somewhere that bagged salad is usually in the supermarket within 48 hours of being picked. Two days! Grow it yourself and cut it down to two minutes.

The simplest way to grow locally adapted vegetable varieties is to save seed from open-pollinated veges that grow well for you and grow them again. It takes time, but plants do adapt genetically to local conditions.

Right plant, right place

This is the one gardening rule worth remembering. If you find a plant that suits the conditions you are giving it, then it stands a much better chance of thriving. But the trick is to look at your garden and assess the conditions on offer and then plant to it, rather than try to manipulate the conditions to grow what you want. The phrase right plant, right place (which is the title of a book by the great British plantswoman Beth Chatto) is often used about ornamental plants but frankly, it's just as useful in the vegetable garden. Beth Chatto suggested you research the plant's native growing conditions, then look for those conditions in the microclimates of your own garden. If your garden does not offer them, move on. But grow what suits your bioregion and your garden will be less work and more productive.

Pick what to grow based on what suits regionally as well as seasonally. That's not to say you will or won't be able to grow a particular vegetable, there are all sorts of varieties of every vegetable, and they perform quite differently in different locations. Buy seeds and plants from local nurseries and seed companies if you can. They will be familiar with the conditions you are growing in: plus, if they have grown something and saved seed from it for a few years, they have hopefully selected for the best chance of success in the local growing conditions. You can also find experienced gardeners who live near you and ask what varieties grow well for them.

If you are growing heirloom crops, I had a good friend who used to focus on heirloom crops that originated in as similar an environment as his garden as possible. You can also seek out hybrid crops that had been bred to cope with the challenges (short summers, humidity, warmer winters, stuff like that) of gardening where you live.

This is not to say you cannot experiment and try growing things that aren't technically possible where you live. I do it all the time. But focus for the most part on the crops that suit the conditions on offer and your vegetable garden will produce a bigger harvest for less work.

There are heaps of local seed saving groups across the country and often they hold regular seed swaps (the pic above is from a winter seed swap in Darfield, Canterbury). These provide a great opportunity to pick up seed varieties that suit where you live.

How much time will it take?

Growing food isn't something you have to spend a lot of time doing. You can, but you don't have to. In their excellent book *The Abundant Garden*, Yotam and Niva Kay from Pakaraka Permaculture in Thames, suggest that maintaining a 10sqm garden will take a beginner gardener 1.5 hours a week, and an experienced gardener 45 minutes a week (they also estimate the yield of the 10sqm plot as being 40-60kg of vegetables for a beginner grower and about 80-100kg for an experienced pro).

I don't know how those figures were worked out, but they sound about right to me. I was talking to Adrian Sutherland, a food grower from Gisborne, about the time you need to spend in the garden the other day. Adrian has a popular social media account "One Minute Gardening" in which he passes on a variety of gardening tips in a minute or less. "Obviously it takes more than one minute to grow food," he told me. "But I wanted to show you could do something in just one minute. Nothing in itself was that complicated. How could it be if it could be explained in one minute?"

Adrian says he had heard from a lot of people who thought being a gardener meant having no life, and no free time. "But it's not true at all," he says. "It's about taking on whatever you can manage. That might be a few buckets, or a couple of tubs with some salad greens. Next season you might get a few more planters and maybe put something in the ground. You just advance from there. People over-complicate it, which stops them trying."

Adrian says a huge benefit of growing food is being able to share it. "I mean a lot of the time we can't keep up with how much we grow," he admits. "So we give boxes of veges to our friends when they come over just to help us get through it. And it works out. I haven't been hunting for years but there's venison in our freezer. Wild pork in our freezer. Crayfish turns up on the doorstep. It all comes around."

A caveat about time:
I genuinely don't think it takes a lot of time to grow food but one thing I would say is if you are putting in an hour a week, you'd be better off doing 10 or 20 minutes every couple of days rather than a 12-hour day every three months. That's one of the reasons I like Adrian's approach: I think you get the best results from a vege garden if you treat it as a lot of little jobs, rather than one big one. So, gardening doesn't have to take a lot of time, but it definitely helps if you are prepared to do it regularly. Little and often will absolutely deliver better results if you really want to eat what you grow.

Salad days

Adrian's wife Bong was born in Vietnam. "And if you know Vietnamese, they eat veges like they are going out of fashion," he says. He, Bong and their toddler daughter Lily Melody love salad, he says: "and when we eat a salad it isn't a token salad. You look at it and think 'are we feeding a horse?'" So they grow a huge range of lettuces and herbs in their 1100sqm Gisborne garden. "When you see those little bags of mixed greens at Pak'nSave? We might eat the equivalent of four or five of those at one time. We're probably eating $20 worth of salad in one go."

Clockwise from top: Lily Melody's first solid food was homegrown kūmara; Lily Melody; Adrian plants into mounds, he finds it produces food more quickly: Adrian Sutherland; new seedlings

Marigolds have been shown to suppress disease-promoting organisms, but if you want to use them for that purpose, you are better planting them as a cover crop in the same spot and about two months before you plant the crop you are trying to protect rather than just growing them alongside your veges at the same time.

Companion planting

Companion planting is the idea that there can be some kind of beneficial symbiotic interactions between plants. Now I am not disputing that plants exist in a complicated and interconnected web of life, they do. But I do challenge a lot of the common companion planting theories that swirl around, they seem to me to be based more on magical thinking than any kind of practical experience. I have heard, more than once, that planting basil next to tomatoes will infuse the tomatoes with the flavour of basil. It won't, and that is a hill I will die on. You can grow them together, I have, but the tomatoes quickly shade out the basil if you are not careful.

Now I am a fan of interplanting (see page 233), also called polycropping, which is growing edible crops alongside each other to make the maximum use of space: usually by sneaking something fast growing in while something slower growing establishes. I also rate planting pollen- and nectar-rich plants – in particular, buckwheat, alyssum and phacelia but I grow calendula, marigolds, nasturtium, borage and chamomile in my vege beds too, as well as letting a variety of vegetables flower and go to seed. This all helps bring in pollinators and useful predatory insects: such as hoverflies, whose larvae devour aphids, mites, scale insects and young caterpillars; parasitoid wasps, which predate on caterpillars; and ladybirds, the adults and larvae of which eat a range of soft-bodied sap suckers.

I also try to grow trap crops, which are plants you grow that are (allegedly) more attractive to the pest you are targeting than the desired crop you are trying to protect. I am not 100 percent sure how effective that technique is, to be honest, I am still experimenting. But I think they are useful in that, if you have something you don't plan to eat and it gets a few aphids or caterpillars, it attracts the beneficial predators that help protect what you do want to eat. You have to be able to tolerate some minor infestations to get the benefit of the beneficials. Try cleome and calendula to attract green vege bugs, nasturtium for aphids, marigolds for nematodes, and chervil for slugs.

This season I am going to plant flowering tobacco, or *nicotiana*, near my tomatoes since Anthony Tringham from Curious Croppers, heirloom tomato growers in Clevedon, Auckland, told me there is an endemic polyphagous mirid that thrives on flowering tobacco and which absolutely wipes out the tomato-potato psyllid.

Finally, there are a lot of theories about plants that repel pests. And it is true that some plants have evolved to have defence mechanisms against pests: garlic, for instance, produces an organosulfur compound, allicin, when the tissues are crushed as a defence against pathogens and pests. So, people say, grow it under your roses to protect against aphids. But the thing is the release of the allicin is triggered by damage to the plant (that's literally why you crush garlic when you are cooking, allicin is one of the chemicals responsible for its flavour). It doesn't release it all the time as it's growing. I don't think growing garlic near roses would make any difference to your aphid issues.

I'm not saying there aren't plants you can use to deter pests. There are. But the only one I have seen peer-reviewed science about is using marigolds to suppress soil-dwelling nematodes (marigolds actually are a trap crop for nematodes, they attract them but also produce a chemical that affects the ability of nematodes to reproduce. But even then you'd need to use them as a cover crop to get the benefit). There absolutely might be more peer-reviewed science I have not seen.

But I have a small garden and don't have much choice but to grow all sorts of things in it, cheek by jowl. Everyone seems to get along fine. So feel free to companion plan to your heart's desire, and confine your vegetables to friendship groups like they are at a slumber party. But I think you are far better growing as big a range of plants as you can in the space you have. Diversity above the soil equals diversity below the soil, and if you look after your soil, all plants can be friends, I say.

Plant guilds are a kind of companion planting I suppose: grouping plants to perform different functions around a food plant. You might include a nitrogen fixer, something to attract good bugs, something with a tap root and a ground cover. I like this and try to do it under fruit trees.

Clockwise from top left: Amaranth; butterflies are attracted to red, yellow and orange flowers; pansies; 'Hughey' broad beans in flower.

This is an F1 hybrid chilli in my garden. No stress if you want only to focus on open-pollinated vegetable varieties so you can save seed. But don't automatically assume an heirloom is superior to a hybrid, or vice versa. And if you are dealing with a particular challenge (short summers or a windy spot or something like that), look for hybrids bred to deal with those conditions.

Hybrid vs heirloom

Heirloom vegetables are open-pollinated, non-hybridised vegetable varieties. There are a lot of different measures for how old a seed needs to be an heirloom, but generally it has been grown for 50 years at least, sometimes longer. Heirloom vegetables are true to type, which means they produce seeds that will, if planted, produce something pretty much similar to the parent plant.

Hybrid vegetables are the result of a deliberate cross between two different plant parents, one specific cultivar pollinating another specific cultivar usually in order to combine desirable qualities (such as colour, flavour, disease resistance, yield) from the two parents into one plant. That first cross is known as an F1 or first filial generation hybrid and that first generation produces offspring that are uniform and vigorous – literally because of heterosis aka hybrid vigour. But the seed the F1 generation produces is not true to type. If it is viable (hybrids can be sterile), then it will produce something where the available genetic material is combined in different, new and possibly not as good ways. Think of it like people (who are, for the purpose of this argument, hybrids). You receive traits from both your parents – your mother's hook nose, say, and your father's curly hair. But you might also get short, stumpy fingers from some long-forgotten stumpy-fingered relative in the distant past. Your sibling who is created from the same well of genetic potential, has a selection of different qualities arranged in different ways.

When I started growing veges, I was obsessed with heirloom crops and turned my nose up at the idea of growing hybrids. But I have to say over the years I have changed my view and I now grow both. Heirlooms can be great fun, they often have tremendous romance and I love crops I can save seed from myself. But hybrids have often been bred for better disease resistance and increased productivity and neither of those are qualities a gardener can afford to sniff at. Indeed, when I have grown an heirloom and a hybrid variety of the same vegetable side by side the difference has been quite profound especially with tomatoes.

I was talking to Jack Hobbs, from Auckland Botanic Gardens, about this very thing and he agreed it was hard to beat the best F1 tomatoes for performance. People talked about the better flavour of heirlooms, heirloom tomatoes in particular, he said. But the real flavour in tomatoes came not from the sugars (although they are important) but from the flavour volatiles. "And the volatile compounds are lost when tomatoes are put in cold storage," he pointed out. "People buy tomatoes from the supermarket and think the flavour is not as good as the ones they used to pick off their grandmother's plant. But that's because they have been chilled rather than because they are necessarily an inferior-tasting tomato."

Research has isolated the volatile compounds in tomatoes and shown that the flavour of the best hybrid tomatoes was up there with the best heirloom varieties, he told me, "and the best of the F1s are far superior when it comes to plant health and productivity, and right up there when it comes to flavour."

A standard spade has a blade that is a rectangle shape with a sharp edge. It's a good choice if you are working in moderately friable soil. If you're breaking up hard, compacted ground, use a pointed spade, which is basically the shape of a sharp-edged teaspoon.

Soil is everything

Healthy soil is the most essential part of vegetable growing success. Any soil can be improved and time you put into your soil is never wasted.

The more I have learned about soil, the more I realise how little I truly understand it.

used to think I could see the equivalent of perhaps a pixel of, say, the Sistine Chapel. Now, I realise it's more like a pixel of the entire Milky Way. You could write a dozen books on soil and not even begin to convey the complexity and importance of the world beneath our feet. Suffice it to say that life could unequivocally not exist without soil and good soil is the heart of success in the garden, indeed it is probably the kidneys, liver, brain, lungs and all the other organs too.

Soil is made up of small particles of rocks and minerals, water, air, organic matter (which means the decomposing remains of anything that was, or was produced by, a living organism, including plants and animals). All soil contains silt, clay and sand although the ratio of one to another varies wildly. There are living organic creatures there too: bacteria, fungi, algae, worms, mites, ants and many, many more. And all of it exists in a complicated and interconnected web of life where everything is connected and communicating and sharing resources.

So yeah, it's complicated.

But that's not to say you should not try and learn more about your soil, you should. The more you understand it, the more you can tactically concentrate your efforts to improve it.

A few years ago, I was talking to the microbiologist Dr Heather Hendrickson, who was then a senior lecturer in molecular bioscience at Massey University, about the life in soil and the incredible range of microscopic fungi, nematodes, protozoa and bacteria that dwell there.

There is one soil bacterium called *Mycobacterium vaccae*, commonly referred to as *M. vaccae*. Heather told me that when you come into contact with this particular bacterium, your serotonin levels increase.

This was discovered because *M. vaccae* is related to *Mycobacterium tuberculosis*, the causative agent of tuberculosis, and scientists wanted to see if *M. vaccae* had any therapeutic medicinal applications. So, they gave it to patients who were suffering with some incurable disease and the patients reported that it improved their mood.

So, they went on to test the bacterium on mice and found that it made mice better at solving mazes. Heather also told me studies had found that children who were exposed to soil had lower rates of asthma and allergies in adult life than children who had not been exposed to soil as much.

So anyway, science shows that getting your hands in the soil means you will be happier, healthier, smarter and less stressed and that does not surprise me in any way at all.

Healthy soil doesn't just support life, it is alive. Microbiologist Heather Hendrickson told me it's estimated there are anything between 2000 and 830,000 different species of microbes alone in every gram of soil.

Compost is a great soil amendment but it's not actually soil. When you mix it into soil and it breaks down completely, compost becomes humus, which is the organic matter in soil.

What kind of soil do I have?

If you are starting a garden and you want to find out what kind of soil you are starting with, the first thing you need to do is get up close to it. There are some very simple soil tests you can do yourself, without any special knowledge or equipment. You can do just one of these, but, if you can be bothered, do them all. I guarantee every minute you put into your soil will pay off exponentially when it comes to your harvests.

DIY Soil Test One

Pick up a handful of soil where you plan to grow your veges and squeeze it, then open your hand. If when you open your hand the soil you are holding crumbles apart, your soil is sandy. If it sticks together in a solid sausage even when you poke it, you have clay soil. If it sticks together at first but then falls apart when you poke it, you have loam soil, which is the holy grail, that's what we are all aiming for.

Loamy soils have it all: they retain water and nutrients around plant roots where it is needed, but still drain well so there's enough oxygen there for soil life and plant roots. If you have clay soil or sandy soil, your aim is to transform it into loamy soil. If you have loamy soil, your aim is to make it loamier. I'm not sure if loamier is a word? But anyway, when it comes to soil, we want all roads to lead to loam.

DIY Soil Test Two

Dig down a little (below anything like mulch that is sitting on top of soil and a little below the surface, you want to test the soil where the roots of the plants would be) and take another handful of soil and put it in a big jar, then top off with water. Put the lid on and shake it up completely then leave it to settle.

Sand particles are the biggest and heaviest particles in soil: ranging from 0.05 to 2mm in diameter. So, they will settle on the bottom of the jar first. Silt particles are the next biggest, 0.002 to 0.05mm in diameter, so they settle

If soil smells sour, it can be because the pH is low. Confirm it with a pH test, they are easy to buy at the garden centre or box store. If your soil smells like ammonia, or bleach, it's usually a sign of bad drainage.

next, but it takes an hour or two. Clay particles are the smallest of all, smaller than 0.002 mm, so they hang about for ages suspended in the water, making it cloudy. But if you leave the jar undisturbed for long enough, you'll have clear water at the top and then layers of soil, silt and clay that give you an idea of the ratio of the three in your soil. It can take a while though, when I did this for the first time at my place, which is heavy volcanic clay, it took a couple of days for the clay layer to settle.

You can measure each layer, add the height of all three layers and work out what percentage is sand, silt and clay. Then use the soil texture triangle opposite to determine the texture class of your soil. It has the sand percentages on the bottom, the clay percentages on the left and the silt percentages on the right. Just draw a line at the percentage of sand, clay and silt in your soil and the point where the lines intersect gives you an idea of what kind of soil you are working with.

DIY Soil Test Three, Four and Five

There are three soil tests you can start in the same way, which is by digging a decent-sized hole. Aim for one that's about the size of a regular bucket, or a little bigger.

First, dump all the soil that you have dug out to make the hole onto a piece of cardboard or in your wheelbarrow and root through it with a trowel or something to see how much life is in it. Count the number of earthworms. If you find five worms or fewer, there's not much organic matter in your soil. If you find between six and 15, you have a decent amount of organic matter, if you find 15 or more the level of organic matter is high and over 30 it is exceptionally high and bursting with goodness and life.

But that's the goal, you don't need to start there. Repeat the same test over subsequent years and hopefully see the worm count and soil life increase. The worm census is a test you want to do in spring, when the soil is damp but not wet. If you do it when your soil is very dry, or very cold, then the earthworm numbers will be radically lower.

Now look back at the sides of the hole you just dug. You should be able to see a dark layer on the top (topsoil) and the paler layer below (subsoil). This is a particularly useful one to do if you are starting a garden on a new build as often developers do things like scrape off the topsoil. The colour of the soil tells you a lot: loamy soil will be brown, like chocolate; sandy soil will be paler tans and yellows; while clay soil is typically redder or dark grey.

If the soil is paler grey and sour-smelling, then it is likely to be waterlogged and needs to be opened up before you can plant in it. If you can see a reddish-brown horizontal line, it could be hard pan, which is an all but impermeable layer of compacted soil that nothing will be able to grow through and that you will need to break through (you can do so slowly by adding organic matter or quickly, but much more manually, by punching through it with a digging fork).

Soil texture and soil structure are not the same. Soil texture is the shape or feel of soil, soil structure is how soil particles join together and the pore spaces that exist between them.

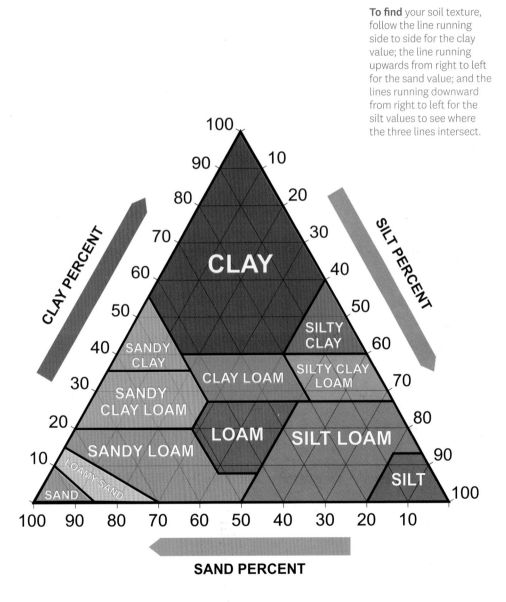

To find your soil texture, follow the line running side to side for the clay value; the line running upwards from right to left for the sand value; and the lines running downward from right to left for the silt values to see where the three lines intersect.

100
90   10
80   20
70   30
CLAY
60   40
50   50
SANDY   SILTY
40   CLAY   CLAY   60
SANDY   CLAY LOAM   SILTY CLAY
30   CLAY   LOAM   70
SANDY
20   CLAY LOAM   80
LOAM   SILT LOAM
10   SANDY LOAM   90
LOAMY SAND   SILT
SAND   100

100 90 80 70 60 50 40 30 20 10

CLAY PERCENT

SILT PERCENT

SAND PERCENT

Soil texture is determined by the ratio of sand, silt and clay. Soil texture affects soil's water-holding capacity, permeability, and workability.

Clockwise from top left: Test drainage; get to know your soil; count worms; measure pH.

There's an incredible variation in the colour of soil and, by observing the colour, you can learn a lot about the mineral composition, trace element concentration, percentage of organic matter and moisture content. If you want to really nerd out, the Manaaki Whenua Landcare Research has a soil colour chart on the soil portal of its website (the colours of soils are named and described by what is called the Munsell colour system, basically like a Pantone colour chart or paint-sample card, but for soil). It gets pretty complicated but it's very useful if you want to compare your soil over time. Even if you keep notes it's very hard to remember exactly what you meant by yellowish-red or greyish-brown any distance of time later.

The final test is to fill the hole with water. After that water has drained away, fill it again and measure (with a ruler) the distance of the water to the very top. Check about a quarter of an hour later to see how much the water has drained. Ideal soil drainage is about 5cm an hour (so if your soil has drained by 1cm in a quarter of an hour, it's draining at 4cm an hour if that makes sense), but anything between 2.5cm and 7cm is OK for most plants. If your soil drains more slowly than 2.5cm in an hour, then it is heavy, and you'll need to improve the drainage. On the other hand, if your soil drains more quickly than 7cm an hour then it is very free-draining, and you need to build up its moisture-holding capacity.

Extra for experts: other soil tests

There are other soil tests you can buy equipment to do, or cause to have done. You can buy a soil pH test at any garden centre or box store, which is interesting to know about and quite easy to do. You can also buy combined pH and moisture meters, which give you a measure of the moisture content in your soil at the same time. You can pay for a microbial assessment of the biological life in your soil, and/or its chemical composition if you want to (you don't have to, and I never have, but I know gardeners who have done and it's very interesting to see the results). And Soilsafe Aotearoa offers a free soil test to anyone in New Zealand, which will show you the concentration of heavy metals and contaminants (such as lead, arsenic and mercury) in your soil. Hours of fun to be had.

The optimal pH for vegetables is 5.5-6.5, but luckily that's not hard to achieve, most soils in New Zealand are slightly acidic.

Building better soil

Step one: add compost

No matter what kind of soil you have, adding compost is
a good idea. Adding compost – aka decomposed organic
material – to your soil is the easiest and simplest thing you
can do to improve how your veges grow. It increases your
soil's ability to hold moisture and nutrients, and improves
your drainage. It adds organic matter to soil that, over time,
is available to feed your plants (fun fact: the organic matter
that is in compost is broken down by microorganisms in
your soil into the bioavailable nitrate and ammonium that
plants can take up, and the time it takes for that to happen
is regulated by temperature, as it happens more quickly
when it is warmer, which is when plants are growing and
so need the energy). Compost contains a huge number
of beneficial soil organisms that help suppress soil-borne
diseases. If you are starting a new garden, add a 5cm
layer of compost to the top. I use something small like
a hand fork to work it into the top layer of the soil. With
existing beds, add a layer of compost a couple of times
a year and work it in (again, a 5cm layer is great if you
have that much compost, but if not just make it a thinner
layer). With plants in pots add a layer of compost to the
soil every three months or so (although you don't need
to add compost to brand new potting mix, see page 245).
Homemade compost is wonderful (see page 46) but if you
don't make it yourself or can't make enough for your needs,
then buy a high-quality compost. But don't skip this step
because compost is key to healthy soil that is full of life.

Step two: mulch, mulch, mulch

Mulch is basically a layer of something you put on top of
soil. It can be something organic that eventually breaks
down, like pea straw or bark: but you can use something
that doesn't break down, such as stones, or something
inorganic, like black plastic, too. Mulching has so many
benefits: it inhibits weeds seeds from germinating, it keeps
moisture in the soil, it insulates the soil, prevents erosion,
stops nutrients from leaching and stimulates invertebrate

If you have sandy soil,
stick to controlled-release
fertilisers. The highly soluble
store-bought fertilisers will
wash straight through sandy
soil and be wasted.

If you are buying compost, it's much, much cheaper by the trailer load than by the bag, although you do need to wheelbarrow it to where you want it in the garden.

Here are lupins growing as a cover crop in Kath Irvine's Levin garden. The holes in the lupins are where she tucked in new squash seedlings. The trick is to ensure the squash get enough light, she says.

activity. And, of course, if you use something organic as a mulch (which, spoiler alert, I recommend) it adds organic matter to the soil too as it breaks down. I use pea straw in my vege beds, partly because it's a great soil conditioner, getting pulled into the soil over time by worms and improving its structure, but partly because I like the look of it. But you can use bark, wood chips or sawdust, grass clippings or green waste, shredded leaves or seaweed or all of them combined. And you can buy mulch, although once you get your eye in for it there is free mulch everywhere for the taking. You can even use plants as mulch too: either as a green crop (see page 42) or by planting so intensively that every inch of the soil is covered.

You normally see it suggested to mulch in spring: when you can keep the winter rain in the soil and (hopefully) stop a surge of spring weeds. But I think there's no real bad time to mulch (caveat: don't apply mulch to bone-dry soils, it's just as effective at keeping moisture out of soil as keeping it in). I try to apply it in autumn or winter when I can see where I am putting it and any old time after I have cleared an area. Whatever you are using, apply it to a depth of about 5 or 6cm, any deeper and it can form a blanket that smothers rather than protects.

If I am applying mulch somewhere I want to keep the competition from weeds down, like under fruit trees, I often put down a weed barrier under it too. Not weed cloth, which I don't use or recommend, but something opaque that will in time breakdown but inhibit weed seed germination while it does so. I often use bits of scrap cardboard, but I have, at various times, used old cotton towels and sheets, woollen jumpers, scraps of wool carpet, and those woollen insulation liners you sometimes get around frozen food. You might think that would make my place look an absolute tip, but if you pile whatever organic mulch you are using on top of it you don't see whatever you have used as a weed barrier at all.

Step three: leave no bare soil

This is really just an extension of step two, since one great way to cover bare soil is with mulch. But you never see bare soil in nature, and you shouldn't see it in your garden either. You also shouldn't plant edible crops too close together – different crops need different spacing and not giving them enough space will cause lots of problems. But I plant as close together as I can get away with (and often closer than that, I'll admit I am a chronic over-planter). Ideally, you want the plants to cover the soil but not each other, so when fully grown they touch but do not overlap. To avoid bare soil, you want to plant something new as soon as you take something out. You don't have to wait until you have harvested a whole crop of something either, plant bit by bit as you harvest. And finally, fill any gaps with green crops, especially over winter although you can use them over the rest of the year too to fill gaps or provide fast nutrition – so, you might use a nitrogen fixer, like a legume,

If you have clay soil, you can add coarse sand to improve the drainage but don't add fine sand as it can block soil pores.

prior to growing a nitrogen-hungry leafy crop like lettuce or spinach. Green crops are also known as cover crops, green manure or living mulch, fast-growing plants that, while they are growing, cover bare soil and improve soil structure. Before they flower, or definitely before they set seed (most cover crops self-seed pretty easily so if you let them seed they will pop up everywhere), and ideally about three weeks before you plan to plant in that spot, you lop them off at ground level and leave them on top of the soil as a mulch or work them in. There are lots of different cover crops you can use – peas, broad beans, lupins, vetch, phacelia, oats, mustard, buckwheat – and mixes that include several different complementary sorts. All of them protect and improve soil, shielding it from damage from weather, wind and rain as they grow, and raising its fertility and organic matter as they break down. Some send out fibrous roots that help improve drainage, aeration and soil structure too.

Step four: practise crop rotation

Crop rotation basically means shifting certain plant groups each year. Different plants take up different minerals and nutrients, so this stops one crop from denuding your soil of anything in particular. Plus rotating what you grow where each year will minimise the chance of pests and diseases in soil that affect certain plant families having a chance to build up. Crop rotation freaks people out but in its simplest terms you want to think about plant families and avoid growing two plants from the same family in subsequent seasons – especially if they are crops that stay in the ground for a few months.

Here is my own rough and ready four-bed system

In bed one, I grow legumes. So that's runner, climber and broad beans and peas. These are nitrogen fixers.

In bed two, grow leafy crops. That's brassicas like broccoli, cauliflower and cabbage (I don't grow Brussels sprouts in my Auckland garden, but if I did they would be in here), as well as lettuce (which to be honest I pop in all the beds), spinach and silverbeet. These are high users of nitrogen.

In bed three, grow fruiting crops. So that's heat-loving Solanaceae like tomatoes, chillies and capsicums, as well as eggplants, melons, zucchini, pumpkins and cucumbers. I grow corn in this bed too, not that it's a fruit, but it seems to get along fine with them. These plants are all high phosphorus users.

In bed four, grow root crops. That includes garlic, carrots, radishes, beetroot, onions and kūmara. These plants have high potassium needs.

In year two bed one becomes bed two, and bed two bed three and so on. Obviously, this is a pretty flexible system, as I pop things in here and there. Plus, you need a bed five really, for crops that stay in one spot like strawberries, rhubarb, globe artichokes or asparagus, and then there are things I grow out of the beds like potatoes. But in general, try to mix it up as much as you can.

Even if you can't move your entire vege patch, try to leave a three-year gap before growing the plants that are most vulnerable to soil-borne diseases (which is basically brassicas, tomatoes, alliums and potatoes) in the same place.

One of the in-situ worm farms in permaculture teacher Dee Turner's garden in New Plymouth. If you are putting them in at your place, site them near gross feeders, like citrus; or vege plants that stay in the ground for a while, like tomatoes and eggplants.

Learn to love compost

I remember talking with a friend of mine, who was, like me, a very keen gardener, about the principles of permaculture (you can see why I am a popular dinner party guest). Anyway, the sixth principle of permaculture is produce no waste. The aim is for your garden to be a closed loop, or as close to that as possible, where you don't have resources constantly coming in and going out but all the energy that enters the system is captured . He told me he had a personal mantra based on that principle, which was that no organic matter should leave his property. All the organic matter that his garden produced, he said – that is green waste, grass clippings, fallen leaves, pruning, weeds and so on, but also the vegetables he grew then ate and any food scraps left over – was potential energy that could be returned to the garden. And what was more, it had taken energy from the garden already: using nutrients from the soil, as well as capturing energy that came into the garden from the sun and the rain. If he sent all that away in a truck as green waste, he told me, he was simply throwing that energy away. Plus, he would need to waste his own time, energy and possibly money bringing in resources in order to replace it: buying compost to build soil fertility and paying for mulch and so on. This conversation made a big impression on me and I have thought about it a lot since. I know in Auckland half of what is sent to landfill is compostable, it's just crazy to think of all that potential energy being wasted. It's hard to create all the compost you need, I can't myself, but whatever you manage to achieve is worthwhile and you can supplement with bought compost as required. Although if you are buying compost, as with potting mix (see page 245), you get what you pay for. The cheapest ingredient you can buy to make compost and potting mix in New Zealand is municipal garden waste, and there is no way to know if the green waste in that has been treated with any herbicides. If it has been, the herbicides are not removed or rendered inactive through composting. I buy organic compost and always ask what the compost is made from. If it contains municipal green waste, I'd look for another option.

An upcycled worm farm: I was very impressed by these in-situ worm farms that I first saw in Dee Turner's garden. She makes them by taking a 10-litre bucket, cutting the bottom out of it and drilling holes in the side. She buries them so the top is the same level as the soil and uses a terracotta pot saucer as a lid. At the start of every season, she fills the bucket with an animal manure (horse, cow or sheep) then puts a handful of compost worms on top. The tiger worms turn the manure into vermicast, and the earthworms in the beds go in through the holes and take that vermicast out into the soil. You can lift the lid and add food scraps as the season progresses too.

How to compost

There are a lot of ways that you can capture and use the energy in your kitchen and garden waste – trenching, a worm farm or a Bokashi bin. But if you have space, a compost heap is probably the simplest, it really just involves piling organic matter up and hanging around while those helpful organisms break it down for you. Find an out-of-the-way spot, in shade or semi-shade in summer but in sun in the winter if you can manage it (if it's in full sun in summer, the heap can dry out, and all the organisms that decompose organic waste need water, while if it's in shade in winter it can get too cold and if it gets too cold those beneficial composters will stop working). It's better to position the heap directly on soil or lawn, but you can do it on concrete if that's your only choice: it just means that soil organisms can't get into your compost bin to help out. Lay down a layer of branches or stalks first then pile organic matter on top in rough layers, alternating between carbon-rich layers (also called browns) and nitrogen-rich layers (aka greens). You want about two to four parts brown materials for every one part green materials, but it's not an exact science. Carbon-rich materials include straw, sawdust from untreated wood, cardboard and paper, dried leaves and woody prunings. Nitrogen-rich materials include grass clippings, vege scraps, garden waste, tea leaves, coffee grounds, manure, even weeds (but don't compost any seedheads from weeds or perennial weeds that regrow from pieces of roots or stems). Avoid meat and bones, bread, cooked food, dairy, cooking oil and glossy printed paper or cardboard. Try to keep the pieces of whatever you are adding on the small size to increase the speed of decomposition: cutting or shredding the material into small pieces gives the microorganisms more surface area to work on. You want the pile to get to a cubic metre or so, at least, so that heat can build up (it literally gets hot because of how hard all those useful organisms are working to break everything down, but the heat renders non-viable any weed seeds as well as certain plant diseases). Finish with a brown layer and throw a tarp or an old piece of carpet over the top. The useful composters you want need oxygen too, so turn the heap now and again to help get air into it; although that's a hard and heavy job so I often just use a compost aerator, which is like a giant corkscrew. In about six months you should have finished compost but the time of year makes a difference, it breaks down more quickly in spring and summer and slower in winter. The ratio of carbon to nitrogen is pretty forgiving, but if you get too much nitrogen then you know it: the compost goes from breaking down aerobically (as in it is being broken down by microorganisms that need oxygen) to breaking down anaerobically (by microorganisms that do not need oxygen). If it's breaking down anaerobically, it will be slimy and smelly. If that happens, just add more carbon-rich brown material.

I love trench composting. Just dig a trench that's about 45-60cm deep, cover the base with kitchen waste and vege scraps, and back fill so there's about 30cm or so of soil on top.

Compost choices There are loads of home-composting set-ups, from the classic Dalek-shape to the traditional triple bay (one bay for filling, one bay where compost is resting and one bay of compost for using). You can buy tumbling composters, which you turn to get air into the compost, but they are enclosed so earthworms and beneficial soil bacteria can't get in to help out. Plus, if you want to make compost, you would be better filling them in one go, rather than adding organic material that hadn't broken down to compost that is nearly ready. If you want something you can keep adding green waste and kitchen scraps, I'd say a worm farm would be a better choice; the worm castings and worm wees are both great for the garden.

Clockwise from top: Dalek bin; the classic triple bay; a basic wire cylinder; a tumbling bin.

Clockwise from top left: Starting out; the no-dig beds; Candy Harris; the layers of organic matter.

To dig or not to dig?

No-dig gardening is, in very simple terms, gardening without tilling or cultivating the soil in order to preserve soil structure and minimise the disturbance to underground life. It's been around for a long time, but it's been hugely popularised in the last few years, especially by the British author and vegetable grower Charles Dowding who has been experimenting with the technique for the last 40-odd years in his garden, Homeacres, in Somerset, England.

Rather than till or dig the soil to remove weeds, break up soil and aerate your beds, with no-dig gardening you just pile more and more organic matter (such as mulch or compost) on top. The theory is that's what happens in nature: plants and animals drop organic matter all over the soil, and both eventually die and decompose. That organic matter gets incorporated back into the soil thanks to the multitude of different soil organisms that break it down. All of those lifeforms are part of a complex interconnected ecosystem and that ecosystem works most effectively when it is kept intact; whereas when you dig the soil you destroy it.

I am a no-dig gardener myself, partly by circumstance, as much of my vegetable-growing area is in raised beds that are at a height that makes digging awkward. But my friend Candy Harris who has a 1000sqm edible garden in Clarkville, Waimakariri, created a no-dig bed a couple of years ago: scraping off the grass, covering the area with cardboard and newspaper, then piling all the organic matter she had on hand in layers, alternating green layers with brown layers (see page 46) until the beds were about 30cm high. Then she added a layer of compost to the top and covered that with a pea straw mulch and planted seedlings straight into it. Carrots did better in her main garden, which she was still digging, she told me, but everything else did as well or better in the no-dig bed.

You can use the exact same technique on top of an existing garden bed if you want to revive the soil in it too. Think of it as making compost in situ, rather than making it elsewhere in the garden and hauling it from one place to another.

Getting started
Candy started her no-dig garden by defining beds using plastic weedmat to make paths. She's not a fan of weedmat in general, and isn't sure if she will use it in her next no-dig beds, but needed to stop Kikuyu grass getting into the beds.

What about fertiliser?

The primary way you want to build soil fertility is by adding compost and organic matter. But most vege crops are fast-growing annual crops, which take up nutrition from the soil very quickly, and if there is not enough food for them, they will fail to perform. In my garden, I use broad-spectrum organic fertilisers and mineral fertilisers judiciously to support their growth.

Fertilisers are basically concentrated sources of the nutrients that plants need to grow. The three key nutrients in them are nitrogen, to promote green growth and foliage; phosphorous, which promotes healthy root growth; and potassium, which supports flowering and fruiting. If you look on any pack of bought fertiliser you will see an N:P:K ratio, which is the ratio of those three nutrients.

They also often contain the other macronutrients – calcium, magnesium and sulphur – that plants need to grow, and trace elements that plants need but only in tiny amounts – iron, chlorine, copper, manganese, zinc, molybdenum and boron.

There are organic fertilisers and fertilisers that are synthetic or inorganic. I used to use both sorts but for several years now I have only used organic fertilisers, which basically means fertilisers that are made from plants (seaweed, comfrey tea), minerals (dolomite lime) or animals (blood and bone, sheep pellets).

Organic fertilisers tend to break down more slowly over time, whereas synthetic fertilisers deliver nutrition to your plants that they can access instantly. Think of the latter like Uber Eats – fast but maybe not the best for long-term health.

And although plants do not distinguish between the nutrients in the organic and artificial sorts in any way, artificial fertilisers have a terrible impact on all those microscopic fungi, bacteria and animals that live in the soil and do so much to benefit its structure and inherent fertility.

Whatever you are using, only apply it so it can be used by your plants when they need it, which is when they are actively growing. I usually apply a broad-spectrum organic fertiliser in autumn so the nutrients in it can be broken down by the life in the soil and available in a usable form for what I plant in spring. If I forget to do it in autumn, I add it as early as possible in spring. Then I top up with liquid fertilisers over spring and summer. I also use a bit of dolomite lime, which is a mix of calcium carbonate and magnesium carbonate (although don't do that if your soil is alkaline) and rock phosphate.

And finally, I use worm wees, comfrey tea and homemade seaweed teas regularly over the growing season. They contain some of the nutrients that plants need but they are nothing like as strong as bought fertilisers. They are more like a general health tonic that helps build your plants' resilience and increases the microbial life in the soil. So really worth doing and highly recommended but not the same as or a substitute for fertilising.

Dr Jessica Hutchings
is a Hua Parakore (Māori organic) food grower on a small whānau farm in Kaitoke. Hua parakore is a kaupapa Māori system for growing kai. Jessica applies liquid fertiliser to all the garden beds. She also foliar sprays with different fertilisers once a week.

If you save seed, you have loads. I always pick the biggest seed to grow on. The theory is larger seed contains more resources to start plants off on the best foot.

Grow more plants

Propagation is one of the
most fun things about vege
gardening for me, so do try
sowing seeds, dividing plants,
and growing from cuttings.

I sometimes think gardeners make plant propagation sound more complicated than it is.

was talking the other day to Jodi Roebuck who, with his wife Tanya Mercer, runs the astonishingly productive market garden Roebuck Farm in Omata, Taranaki.

Jodi told me he had been round at his mum's place recently to record an episode of his podcast, *The Profitable Mini Farm*, because she has a better internet connection. His mum asked what the show was going to be about that day, and Jodi said it was an hour-long show about growing carrots. And she asked how he could possibly fill a whole hour on carrots when all you had to do was sow them and harvest them. "And she's actually right," Jodi pointed out.

I agree with you, Jodi's mum. Propagating plants is really not that hard. Plants need water, food, oxygen, light and the right amount of warmth. Seeds respond to moisture and temperature always and light some of the time. (Fun fact: not every seed needs light to germinate. For instance, tomatoes and peppers don't, they just need warmth and moisture so they will germinate fine in a dark hot water cupboard, although you need to shift them into the light the second they strike or they will get leggy. Most lettuce seed, on the other hand, is photodormant and will not germinate at all if it is not exposed to light).

Plant propagation is simply the multiplication or production of plants. In my vegetable garden, I start a lot from seed, which is easy and fun, and you don't need any fancy gear or special training. I also grow a bit from cuttings and divisions, neither of which are especially difficult either. There are other ways you can propagate plants, such as layering, grafting and budding, but seeds, cuttings and divisions are the main ones I use at home.

And, of course, if you want more plants you can buy plants from your local nursery or garden centre. I do that too. That is a great choice if you have left it too late to start from seed or you can't be bothered with the fussing about that is required over the seedling phase.

It's also worth considering with crops that are perennial (page 72), or with crops where you only want one or two plants a year (which will depend on you of course, but for me that might be celery because I don't use much of it).

But basically there's no wrong way to increase your plant stock. Play around, try them all, find what works for you. In general, I find it helps in the garden to remember that everything wants to grow. Frankly, just give your edible crops the conditions they like and get out of their way.

Jodi Roebuck,
Tanya Mercer and
their dog Tariq
on Roebuck Farm
in Taranaki.

Give old punnets and pots a good clean before reuse to prevent transferring plant pathogens from the previous season, although the most common problem with seedlings, damping off, is more likely to be caused by plants' growing conditions.

How to succeed from seed

Use seed raising mix

Whether you are starting seed in seed trays, propagation trays, jiffy pots or recycled plastic punnets, use a high-quality seed raising mix. Yes, it is more expensive than general potting mix, but it's a false economy to use that instead. Definitely don't use garden soil, which is very likely to contain fungal spores and weed seeds, plus garden soil can be heavy and claggy because the soil particles in it are packed close together, so it's harder for the delicate roots of a newly germinated seed to push their way through.

Seed raising mix, on the other hand, is light and fluffy because there's lots of air between the particles. In fact, Scott Bromwich, who's on the team at Daltons, a New Zealand company headquartered in Matamata that makes a whole range of growing mediums along with various other horticultural products, told me that seed raising mix is the fine fraction of potting mix that has been sieved off, which ensures the optimum particle size for the germination and growth of seedlings plus a few additions for seedling health.

A good seed raising mix is pathogen- and weed-free, which is helpful as it means you know that any plant that appears is likely to be the one you wanted. It will contain something like pumice or vermiculite for drainage, a wetting agent or water-holding crystal so it holds water around plant roots, gypsum to promote strong root growth and a suitable starter fertiliser that's gentle enough not to burn your newly germinated seeds. Look for one that also contains a fungicide or (even better) is inoculated with beneficial fungi such as Trichoderma to help prevent damping off. Buy fresh mix every season. I know, I know it's expensive and it's tempting to hold onto it, but it doesn't store well and if it gets wet the fertiliser in it will start to be released.

It's possible to make seed raising mix. I have done in the past. But if you are getting started or have had mixed results starting from seed in trays before, I'd recommend you buy it. A good seed raising mix really will do three-quarters of the heavy lifting for you when it comes to starting edible crops from seed.

After you have filled your seed tray or punnet with seed raising mix, tap the whole container on the bench or something to settle the mix and then top up as needed.

Temperature is everything

I think timing is the thing that new gardeners most often get wrong: as in, they sow and plant things when it is not yet warm enough for what they are growing. I see the temptation to trying to get a head start on the season and get stuff in a little earlier, and have 100 percent fallen foul of it myself. But to reduce your mahi load and increase your harvests, wait, wait, wait until the conditions are right for what you are trying to grow. Before you sow and plant – anything at all – ask yourself one important question: is it too early?

Different plants need different conditions to thrive – radically different at times. A study at Lincoln University found the excellent beneficial-insect-attracting herb phacelia, or purple tansy, would generate reliably 12 months of the year, even when soil was frozen. Whereas tomato seed will germinate best if the soil temperature is above 20°C and watermelon seed prefers soil to be 25°C. (Once they have germinated, seedlings can handle a wider temperature range, tomatoes seedlings for instance can be planted when the soil is about 16°C, and watermelons when it's about 20 or 21°C).

The topic of timing when it comes to sowing and planting gets people really riled up, I don't know why. I write a monthly column for *NZ Gardener* about what to sow and plant in the vegetable garden and if I say something about holding off on planting tomatoes seedlings until late October or even November I invariably get a email or a call from someone to tell me they planted theirs in August and have ripe tomatoes already. And to that kind of person I have a standard two word response, which is: well done. (I think it's important to celebrate wins along the way, even when people are heading in completely the wrong direction. I like to think, if they keep going, they will catch up eventually.)

The thing is I am not saying that plants and seeds won't grow if you start them before conditions are ideal. The absolutely might. The only thing seed wants to do is germinate and it will do so if conditions make it even marginally possible.

But I am saying they will not grow as well as if they had been planted or sown when conditions were optimal. The seeds will use up a lot of the energy they contain just surviving under suboptimal conditions rather than using it to produce a large and strong root system or a more abundant crop. And as a result, over the course of their life they will prove less robust than a plant that has not come up through struggle street. They are more likely to be affected by pests and diseases. They will produce less leaves or fruit or whatever it is that you harvest from them.

Every seed has an optimal germination temperature range. You should be able to find it on the seed packet, or there's a guide on page 258. Use your soil temperature as your unassailable guide as to when to sow. You want your plants to flourish, rather than just survive.

Seedlings prefer a consistent temperature. That can catch you out if you have a seed tray next to a window where it sunny and warm all day but still gets cold next to the glass at night.

Jodi Roebuck told me the first piece of equipment he suggests a new gardener buy is a cheap soil thermometer. "It doesn't matter where you live or what the season is doing. When you are coming out of winter when the soil gets to 12°C you can plant your cool season stuff. You can put a carrot seed in the ground and you can transplant broccoli. Then when it gets to 16°C you can transplant beans and tomato seedlings. You cannot go wrong if your feedback loop is temperature."

Clockwise from top left: Jiffy pots; mist seedlings; look for good light; keep records!

Light, moisture and depth

Whatever you are growing, the consistency of the seed raising mix or soil outside should feel like a wrung-out kitchen sponge: moist to the touch but not wringing wet. Never let it dry out completely.

Seedlings cannot store much water and, whether they are growing undercover or directly in the garden, their roots are still very near the surface of the soil, which dries out quickly (especially outside if there is wind). So the seed raising mix or the soil that they are growing in needs to be consistently moist. Inside, I'd suggest watering everyday for the first few weeks, after that it might only be needed every other day. In the garden obviously rain might do some of the watering for you, but the soil outside is exposed to a lot more drying variables so you will still need to keep a very close eye on just-sown seed to ensure there is consistent moisture.

A very basic rule of thumb when it comes to how deep to plant a seed is to sow about twice as deeply as the diameter of the seed. So the smaller the seed is, the more shallowly it needs to be covered. With small seed I just sprinkle it on the top of the mix in the tray and then sieve more seed raising mix on the top so the seed is covered but not buried, if that makes sense – it's a bit like sieving icing sugar onto a sponge cake.

Until seed germinates, I keep seed trays out of direct sun but in good light (I define good light as a spot where there is enough light to read easily). But as soon as germination has occurred, I move them into the brightest spot possible. Most vegetable seedlings need at least 12 hours of light a day to grow into strong robust plants and if they are not getting enough light they tend to strain towards the available light there is and become leggy and weak. Aim for multi-directional light if possible, but if they are by a window or in a situation where the light all comes from one direction, then turn the seed tray or whatever you are growing them in a quarter turn every day to ensure the light falls on all the seedlings evenly.

I can't stress this enough, keep records of what you are sowing at the same time as you are sowing it. Whether you write on those little plant labels or detail it in your garden diary, up to you, just write it down somewhere immediately. You might think you will remember what you have sown where. I guarantee you will not.

Dr Jessica Hutchings has 13 vege beds, and two polytunnels on her whānau food farm Papawhakaritorito in Kaitoke. "We don't buy produce anymore, we are food sovereign on the farm. We do a lot of polycropping, or intercropping, and produce heaps of food. Chopping and dropping and polycropping means you don't have to get out there everyday to keep your garden tidy."

Troubleshooting seeds

I'm going to go out on a limb here and say most vegetables grow pretty easily from seed. Parsnips can be a bit tricky but apart from them, if you sow seed and nothing appears, first look inward and honestly ask yourself... are you to blame? Did you sow too deeply? Is it too cold? Did it dry right out? Or, alternatively, was it in sodden soil (in which case many seeds will rot).

Other than that, the main problem that people have with seed that has been sown inside is a fungal problem called damping off where seedlings start to look fuzzy and mouldy, then rot at the soil line and collapse. There's no coming back from it, and seedlings that are affected cannot be saved. Like all fungal problems, damping off is more like to occur if plants are overcrowded, ventilation is poor, the growing medium is kept too wet and/or drainage is inadequate. You can help by using fresh, pathogen-free seed raising mix, making sure your seed-raising trays or recycled pots or punnets are cleaned before you reuse them and not overcrowding the seedlings of whatever you are growing. Years ago I read a suggestion from the British ethnobotanist James Wong to water or mist with (cold) chamomile tea (chamomile has all sorts of antifungal properties) as a preventative against damping off, and since then I have done that, when I remember to, too.

If you are growing seed outside of course, a few more things can go wrong at that vulnerable early stage. But many problems can be swerved by protecting seedlings while they get established. Make or buy a grow tunnel to cover a whole row – it can be as simple as some no. 8 wire and a sheet of polyethylene. You can also cut the bottoms off old plastic bottles and place them over the top of individual plants. Using the top half means you can take the lid of the bottle off: that allows some ventilation to occur (effectively the bottle acts as a mini hothouse, and if it is entirely closed up then your seedlings can get absolutely fried on a hot day). When the new plant is established and the leaves are starting to touch the sides of the bottle, take the bottles off to use elsewhere or store for the following season.

Newly sown seed is vulnerable to everything. Slugs and snails eat anything that grows; rats, mice and birds dig up and eat seed (especially nutrient-dense beans, peas and corn). At my place, Dusty Springfield (above) goes and lies on top of just emerged seedlings. There is risk everywhere.

Seed-sowing: next steps

If you start seed inside, you will eventually need to prick it out, pot it on or plant it out. Pricking out is when you transfer seedlings growing together into their own plugs or pots to grow on some more before you plant them out. It's a bit of a faff, and if I can get away with it I prefer to start seed in its own pot, which it can stay in until it's of a suitable size to go into the garden. But sometimes you can't avoid this stage, so if you are pricking on, take the opportunity to discard any seedlings that are not growing strongly. I always want to save every single one myself but harden your heart.

I normally wait to prick out seedlings until they have two (or more) true leaves. But interestingly, Yotam and Niva Kay from Pakaraka Permaculture in Thames in their excellent book *The Abundant Garden*, suggest that pricking out seedlings at the cotyledon leaf stage will result in a better root structure (the cotyledon leaves are the first leaves or seed leaves that a plant produces, which often look nothing like the leaves of the mature plant; the true leaves are the next leaves, which do look like the mature leaves). I am going to try pricking on earlier, as they suggest, this spring.

Take considerable care handling seedlings at any stage but particularly that first transplant. Ease them out of the tray (I use a pencil or the non-spoon end of a teaspoon) and tease them apart if they are close together, keeping as much of the growing mix around the roots as you can.

Hold each seedling by a leaf rather than the stem (the stems are very delicate and it's easy to pinch right through them). Use a dibber, your finger, the end of a teaspoon or a pencil to make the hole you plan to plant the seedling in before you lift it so you can drop it straight in and then firm the soil around the roots lightly with your fingers or the spoon end of the teaspoon. Once you have pricked everything on, water the seedlings in their new pots or plugs.

Potting on is when you move seedlings from a small pot or a plug tray into bigger pots. You need to do this with things that take quite a long time to grow big enough to plant outside and/or edible crops that are particularly tender and can't grow outside until it's properly warm like tomatoes and eggplants – you have to grow them on for so long inside that they can exhaust the nutrition available in the soil in a plug tray.

Planting out is when you plant your seedling outside in the garden (or wherever its permanent home might be).

If you are growing heat-loving or tender seedlings (like tomatoes or basil) you need to put them through a process called hardening off before you can move them from growing inside to growing outside. That is effectively introducing them to the outside world gradually. A week or two before you plan to plant them, place them outside for an hour or two in a sheltered spot that's out of direct sun. The next day leave them outside a little longer, gradually moving them into more direct sun.

There's often more seed in a pack than you need at once. To keep extra seed in a foil packet fresh, place a piece of paper over the open end and iron over the top of that to reseal it.

Multicell punnets keep the root system of each plant separate.

Upcycling gone mad

There are many *wild* suggestions for what to start seed in. Eggshells! Ice cream cones! Half orange peels! Those are all real but perfectly dreadful suggestions I've seen online. I recommend you use seed trays or propagation trays, or reuse old punnets or pots. Homemade newspaper pots are fine if its something you can plant out quickly, but they can break up before the planting stage if you grow in them for too long. Egg cartons are OK at a pinch but I find the little wells don't hold much soil and so they dry out too quickly. I find jiffy pots considerably better, and those sustainable peat pellets are great too.

From left I use sustainable peat soil pellets a lot; homemade newspaper pots.

This tip came from a woman I met at a garden club: when sowing direct, backfill with compost rather than soil. It will be a different colour to your soil so you can keep track of where your seeds are, and what grows through the compost is likely to be the desired plant as opposed to a weed.

You can also sow seed direct

Sowing direct means starting seed in the garden when you want it to grow. There's a lot I like about sowing direct. For one thing it's much, much less work; you avoid all the pricking out and potting on stages altogether and nothing needs to be hardened off. I also think every transplant causes a plant stress and so there's a good case for letting a plant grow in the same place over the whole of its life.

However, there are downsides to sowing direct worth pointing out too. Seedlings are incredibly vulnerable at the start of their life and literally every living thing in your garden will try and eat them. Seedlings growing outside will have to cope with a lot more variables around temperature and weather than ones that you can cosset in more controlled conditions.

It's also worth remembering that sowing direct is always not the most efficient way to use your available growing space. John Jeavons, in his book *How to Grow More Vegetables*, a classic in the sustainable gardening space, makes the point that seedlings take days or weeks to get to a size where they can be transplanted out into the garden. If you start the crops in trays or pots, you can use your outdoor growing space for something else over that time. That's certainly something to consider if you want to produce the most you can from the space you have.

But I should mention there are certain crops that I recommend always starting from seed: the ones that have a long and delicate taproot like coriander, dill and fennel, as they hate being transplanted and tend to bolt straight to seed if their roots are disturbed.

It's best practice to start all root crops, such as carrots, beetroot and radishes, direct too: although I have to confess I have transplanted beetroot seedlings at home and they have done perfectly alright. But transplanted carrots often end up forked or bifurcated, while parsnips will bolt straight to seed at the slightest provocation. So sow them direct if you possibly can.

Parsnip seed needs to be absolutely fresh so buy a new packet of seed every year or (even better) leave a few plants to grow on for a second year so this biennial plant can flower and self-seed. Parsnip seed won't germinate if the soil dries out, so cover the row with a wooden plank after sowing. Leave it for eight days (parsnip seed is very slow to germinate, taking 10–21 days), then check it every day. Remove the plank once the first seedling shows.

When to buy seedlings

I like sowing seed for lots of reason. Firstly it's much, much cheaper. A packet of lettuce seed costs less than a punnet of lettuce seedlings, and it contains hundreds of (potential) lettuces. There is also a huge range of vegetable varieties that you can grow from seed, far more than you can buy as a seedlings. But starting from seed does take more time and you can miss the window and get behind the ideal schedule – and buying seedlings lets you catch up. Say you didn't get round to sowing tomato seed, so you have no seedlings ready in late October or November. You can still sow seed then, but you are using up part of the growing season so your tomatoes will be later and you might want to buy seedling to plant straightaway. There are some particularly vigorous vegetable hybrids that are only available to commercial growers so you have no choice but to buy them as seedlings if you want to grow them. Seedlings are also quicker to get to harvest, so plant a few if the gratification of your vege garden is feeling a little too delayed for you. Seedlings are also a good option if you have a small garden or a small family – a packet of cabbage seed might contain about 100 potential cabbages, say. That might overwhelm your growing space and your enthusiasm for making sauerkraut. A punnet of seedlings can be a better option in that case.

Fresh is best with seed. There should be an expiry date on the packet. You absolutely can still sow seed after that date, it's just the germination rate might be lower. If you are not sure, do a germination test: just soak a few seeds in a saucer of water for a day or two. If seeds swell and split and a sprout appears, you'll know it's worth sowing the rest of the packet.

A pack of lettuce seed might contain 1000 seeds, far more than you would ever sow at one time. When I sow some, I write that date on the back of the pack and that helps reminds me when I need to sow more to keep plants coming.

Mint strikes easily. If a friend has a good mint plant, ask for a cutting.

Growing cuttings

Honestly if you want a mint plant, just take a stem of mint and pop it in a glass of water on a windowsill, roots should appear in a week or two. I have tried the same thing with other soft-stemmed herbs like basil, lemon balm and oregano: they're less reliable than mint for me, but still probably strike at least half the time. Woody herbs like rosemary and thyme can be grown from cuttings too: cut off a stem that's about 15cm long from new, green growth and plant in a pot filled with cutting mix or propagation mix (which you can buy at the garden centre).

From left: Divided rhubarb crowns; rosemary cuttings.

Dividing perennials

Clumping perennial plants can be propagated by division. At home I mainly use this method for herbs (try it with thyme, broad-leaf chives, oregano, mint, tarragon, lovage, lemongrass and marjoram), but you can also use it with established rhubarb or congested clumps of strawberries. Once plants are established you basically just dig them up in spring or autumn and divide them up into sections, each one of which you can plant individually to increase your plant stock or have plants to give away. Don't do it in the first year or two after you plant - they need two or three years to get established - but once they are up and running, you can divide them every couple of years in spring, as soon as new growth starts to appear. Indeed it's a good idea to do so as if you leave them to their druthers they tend to get woody or start to die off in the middle; dividing means you always have vigorous plants on the go. Soak the soil in the pot or around the plant in the ground first (either use just water or I might use a highly diluted worm wee or a diluted seaweed tonic if I have either one handy). Then tip out of the pot or dig up the whole plant if it's in the ground, trying to keep the roots as intact as possible. Depending on the size of the plant you are dealing with you can use a spade or a trowel or whatever sharp-edged, suitably sized implement you have handy to divide the clump into three or so sections (don't overthink the tool aspect, I have used a butter knife in the past). Make sure each section includes some above-ground and below-ground growth... you need both shoots and roots. Replant as quickly as you can: bigger pieces can go straight back in the garden and smaller pieces can be planted into pots to grow on and plant or give away.

A case for self-seeders

If you leave leafy greens and herbs – try rocket, Asian greens, silverbeet, lettuce, radishes, chamomile, parsley, spinach, coriander, chives and dill – to flower and set seed then more will probably grow without you having to do much at all. I love letting edible crops self-sow. As well as the ones already mentioned, I leave a few biennial root crops (carrots, beetroot and parsnips) in the ground for the second season so they can flower and self-seed; tomatoes and pumpkins can pop-up (often at the wrong time of the year, it's fair to say); while tomatillos have self-seeded so readily at my place that I wonder if they should technically be considered a weed. I was talking to Jack Hobbs, the general manager of Auckland Botanic Gardens the other day, and he said he was letting more and more vege crops self-seed in his garden too. "I have stuff popping up in my garden all the time," he told me. "Pak choi and mizuna in particular, but coriander pops up all over the place, lettuces randomly appear along with corn salad, which I think is much nicer than lettuce. I love it. It's got every benefit you can think of. The flowers will bring all the beneficial insects into your garden. And you get the same again for nothing."

Perennial crops, which include asparagus, globe artichokes, rhubarb, fennel, scarlet runner beans and perpetual spinach, are edibles that you plant once and they regrow every years so you can harvest from them for years to come. They take up space the whole time – an issue if your growing space is limited – but that's the only downside I can think of.

If a crop has set seed, and you want to shift it somewhere else in the garden, cut off the seedheads when they are nearly dry and pop them in a paper bag to dry fully. When the seeds start to fall out from the seedheads naturally, scrunch the paper bag a bit, then shake the contents on the soil where you want that crop to grow, rake in lightly and water.

If you are growing stems on in water you will need to change the water every couple of days.

Growing on from supermarket scraps

If you have bought any kind of vegetable that is sold with the roots on (like spring onions or fancy lettuce), chop the rooted piece off and plant it. You have nothing to lose, basically, and it almost always works for me with spring onions and most of the time with lettuces.

Even if the roots are not attached, you can take the stem ends of things like celery, leeks or bok choy (or any Asian green really) and pop them into water so about a thumb width of the base is covered but the rest of the plant is out of the water. I've done this with the base part of leeks and celery, and they have grown new roots and I have eventually planted them out in the garden. You can do this with the base of lettuces too, even if the roots have been cut off. They don't root as reliably for me as the other edibles mentioned, but they will often produce new leaves, which you can eat.

Speaking of eating leaves, the feathery foliage of carrots, the leaves of beetroot, turnips and even radishes are all edible. So, if you buy these vegetables with the leafy tops on, then plant the tops you cut off. You won't get another root but they will usually grow new foliage. Young beetroot, radish and turnip leaves can be thrown into your salads, while carrot tops can be used like parsley. You are not going to grow a lot, but it's a fun experiment, especially with kids.

Absolutely fresh salad from Ezra Alexander's compact courtyard garden in urban Auckland.

365 days
of salad

Honestly, salad leaves are one
of the easiest crops to grow.
You don't need much space at
all and the range of what you
can throw into a salad is vast.

I believe it is perfectly possible for every person in New Zealand to be salad self-sufficient.

OK in regions with cold winters it takes more planning, and you need access to some undercover growing space in winter to keep pumping out leafy greens. But hey, even nine months a year of salad self-sufficiency is a worthy goal.

And it is simpler than you think. At home I have two self-watering planters that I keep on the back deck. The planters are 50cm long and 20cm wide and I grow about 10 or 12 upright, cut-and-come-again lettuce varieties crammed into each.

Sometimes I sow seed, sometimes I have seedlings that have self-sown somewhere in the garden, which I then transplant, other times I just pick up a punnet of plants at the garden centre or a newspaper-wrapped bundle of Awapuni seedlings at the supermarket. It's more expensive buying seedlings than starting from seed, but look at it this way: the seedlings – usually you get six, sometimes up to nine – often cost less than one lettuce.

The seedlings in my planters are crammed much too close together of course, but since I am picking and eating from the planters all the time, I mainly get away with it. I give the planters a liquid feed every month or so for most of the year although in winter when the plants are growing much slower I might not even do that.

In my small household of two, those two planters easily produce enough leaves for salads, sandwiches and burgers for several weeks. I give them a couple of weeks to get established and then start picking leaf-by-leaf, and there are enough plants there that the ones you pick from have a chance to produce new leaves before you need to pick from them again. I can usually get three harvests from a plant before it starts to lose vigour. The planters are small enough that I can move them into the shade while new plants are establishing, and I keep them in the shade in summer if it gets too hot as lettuce is prone to bolting in hot weather.

You could do this with any old pot or planter. But I can be both lazy and forgetful when it comes to watering, so a self-watering planter is a great choice for salad greens for me (you can buy them or see page 89 for a DIY version). Lots of leafy, salad-y crops like lettuce, kale, spinach, rocket and different Asian greens are all shallow-rooted and do best in that difficult-to-achieve Goldilocks state where the soil is constantly moist but never wringing wet. With lettuces, you want them to grow fast so the leaves are soft and sweet – if they dry out, they are prone to bolting and even if they don't bolt, growth will slow, which makes the leaves start to taste bitter.

We might think of lettuce as a summer salad staple, but actually it is a cool-season crop and does best when it's between 10-20°C. Some varieties are prone to what is called thermodormancy, which means they will not germinate at all if it gets above 25°C.

A gardener's guide to lettuce

There are basically four kinds of lettuce you can grow: crispheads, butterhead, romaine or cos, and loose-leaf.

Crisphead varieties
Crisphead lettuces are hearting lettuces that have crisp leaves wrapped tightly together to form a head. Varieties include 'Great Lakes', 'Canasta', 'Cisco' or try 'Bug Off' (so-called because it's resistant to lettuce aphids). But 'Iceberg' is the one everyone knows and grew up with and, in my case at least, loves: try making an 'Iceberg' salad with fresh peas and shredded mint and dress it with a basic vinaigrette, it's delicious. Crisphead lettuces are a mainstay of commercial producers because they store well and transport well but I tend not to grow them much. They take up more room, the big ones need to be about 40cm apart, and I find them fiddly divas in the garden. If they dry out or it gets too hot the hearts fail to form or they collapse into themselves in an unappetising pool of rot. Plus, and more importantly, you have to harvest a hearting lettuce all at once. I prefer lettuces you can pick leaf by leaf as then a few plants can give you a steady salad supply.

Butterhead lettuces
Butterhead lettuces form a head too, it's just made up of looser leaves so you can still pick them leaf by leaf, or harvest the whole head at once as you choose. The butterhead lettuce you see most often is 'Buttercrunch' but look out for the stunning-looking 'Merveille des Quatre Saisons', 'Summer Queen', 'Tom Thumb' or the similar teeny-tiny 'Tennis Ball' (which I like because one lettuce makes a great salad for two people). Butterhead lettuces have a lovely delicate flavour, but they don't store at all well. If you have bought them from the supermarket and thought they were nothing special, try growing them yourself. I think you will find the flavour is far superior when the leaves have just been picked.

Winter salads I grow lettuce over winter but growth slows to an absolute crawl as the light levels and the temperature drops. I was talking to Jason Ross, an edible landscape designer in Waitati, north of Dunedin, whose garden gets heavy frosts in winter, and he said the key to winter lettuces in colder climates was having decent-sized plants when the growth started to slow: he sows in February and plants in March for winter. He mainly grows lettuce in a polytunnel in winter: repeated frosts can turn outdoor lettuces mushy.

Romaine or cos lettuces

These lettuces also form heads, but they have that elongated upright form and the crunchy, thick leaves with that distinctive midrib: like the lettuce you find in a classic Caesar salad. I like 'Cos' for the big leaves: you can fill the individual leaves with larb or prawn salad for a super-fast meal, or use the big outside leaves instead of buns for low-carb hamburgers. But there are lots of romaine lettuces worth growing: try 'Baby Cos', 'Nero', red-leafed 'Silvia' or the bronzy-red-leafed 'Rouge D'Hiver'. Romaine lettuces are slower-growing than other lettuces but in Joy Larkcom's iconic book *The Salad Garden* she expands on a technique of sowing them very thickly so the leaves grow upright but they don't form hearts and you can pick them leaf by leaf like any cut-and-come-again crop. I love *The Salad Garden*, I read it before I had a vege garden and indeed I think it was a big part of the reason I started one. I still grow 'Little Gem' in Joy Larkcom's honour (it is her favourite lettuce). It's technically a semi-cos, which means it looks a bit like a cross between a romaine and a buttercrunch lettuce, so you can harvest it as baby leaves after a month or so, but if you leave it for another few weeks it forms a loose head.

Loose-leaf lettuces

These grow as rosettes rather than forming hearts. If you can only grow one sort of lettuce (although I can hardly imagine what kind of authoritarian regime would demand such a position), make it a loose-leaf variety. You can harvest the whole plant at once or pick them a leaf at a time. 'Drunken Woman Fringed Head', 'Green Salad Bowl', 'Royal Oak Leaf', 'Lollo Bionda' and 'Lollo Rossa' are particular favourites of mine but there are hundreds of different varieties so mix it up and see what suits your palate and your place. I find these lettuces much slower to bolt than the other types, so they are a better choice over summer and interestingly, a South Island gardener told me years ago she found the loose-leaf lettuce 'Lollo Rossa' the most cold-tolerant lettuce she grew – she claimed it would continue to grow even after being frozen – so they are a good choice for regions with cold winters too.

You can pull a whole lettuce seedling out of the garden and stand it in a glass of cold water, so its roots are submerged. It'll stay crisp and fresh for a few days.

Jurlique Australia's biodynamic farm in South Australia.

Weed eater

I was visiting a biodynamic, organic farm in Adelaide and saw dandelions flourishing. Being helpful, I started to pull them out. One of the owners rushed over to stop me because they were being grown deliberately. The petals, leaves and roots of dandelions are all edible (and used in herbal remedies and skincare), and they are one of many edible weeds you can add to a salad. Try cleavers, plantain, chickweed, speedwell, onion weed or oxalis. Just add a leaf or two to check you like the taste before you harvest on a commercial scale: edible weeds are strongly flavoured.

At Jurlique the flowers are used in biodynamic preparations and the roots in skincare.

Other leafy crops for salads

Of course, lettuces are a staple of the salad bowl but salad crops go well beyond lettuces and true year-round salad self-sufficiency requires a broader range of leafy greens and edible crops. Lettuce look further, you might say. So here are the other leafy edible crops I grow and regularly serve in salads. Of course, I also throw in cucumbers, tomatoes, radishes and all sorts of other things into my salads: just not edible flowers for the reasons I detail on page 93.

Miner's lettuce
Honestly, grow this one. Talk about easy, it self-seeds like a weed. Plant it once and juicy spade-shaped leaves will pop up every autumn thereafter. You can even cook it like spinach.

Corn salad
Another ridiculously easy salad green for winter and spring, and again you only need to plant it once and it will pop up every year – look for it in the garden as soon as you see Easter eggs in the shops. It's also called lamb's lettuce and mache. The green, spoon-shaped leaves are small so it's fiddly to pick but if you can, chop the whole plant off at the base and leave the stem in the ground and more leaves will be produced.

Salad self-sufficiency Salad is a broad category at my place. I throw in herbs, the edible leaves from beetroot and celery, shoots and pinched-out tops from broad beans and peas, all sorts of things.

Rocket
Easy to grow year-round across most of the country although you might want to try it in afternoon shade in summer (it tends to bolt if it's too hot, and the leaves go from pleasantly peppery to mouth-puckeringly bitter if it dries out). Actual rocket is an annual, but let it self-seed and you should have a steady supply coming on. There's also another leafy crop sometimes called perennial rocket, or arugula, which has narrower, spicier leaves.

Silverbeet

Ahhh, silverbeet. We should be writing poetry in praise of this productive, reliable, pest-free crop. It produces across the country, year-round. The baby leaves are tender enough to use in salads and the ones with coloured stems look super jazzy. It self-seeds readily if you let plants flower but if you keep picking leaves, fresh ones will continue to be produced. I highly recommend perpetual spinach, a type of green-leafed, thin-ribbed silverbeet that you can cook like spinach or eat raw as a young leaf. Beetroot is part of the same family as silverbeet, and the baby leaves of beetroot are great in salads. Don't eat the mature leaves raw though, they get too tough.

Spinach

True spinach can be a bit of a diva, it's very sensitive to both day length and heat and will bolt the second you turn your back in summer. For salads, try growing it in a container between autumn and spring and harvesting it at the baby leaf stage. Look out for seed mixes that contain a range of different kinds to keep life interesting.

Kale

Another great autumn and winter salad crop, and a good self-seeder. You can use baby leaves raw in salads, although I usually pick the leaves, cut out the midrib, roughly chop them, then throw in a bowl with olive oil and lemon juice and massage that in for a couple of minutes. It softens the leaves and, I think, makes them taste much better.

Mustard greens

Pick the leaves of this leafy brassica (it's sort of an open-hearted cabbage) while they are small, if you want to eat them fresh in salads, or use them as microgreens. The bigger leaves are perfectly edible but taste very peppery, I like them better cooked.

Chicory & Radicchio

If you like rocket, try chicory. Older leaves of chicory (in New Zealand the red chicories are usually called radicchio, the green ones just chicory) have a very distinctive bitter taste. That might not sound good, but if you like the bitterness of dark chocolate, give this one a grow. The baby leaves are milder, I find the taste peppery. This is a great leafy crop if you like to make salads that contain something sweet like pear or apple slices, pineapple chunks or orange segments, and it's very hardy in cooler places. There are hearting and non-hearting chicories but don't worry too much about it, you can pick all of them leaf by leaf before they heart up.

Tatsoi

There are loads of Asian greens you can grow for salad leaves, but tatsoi and mizuna are my favourites. Just pick the spoon-shaped, white-ribbed leaves while they are young for salads. Tatsoi is incredibly fast- growing but if you miss the window and the plants mature beyond the salad stage, just use the leaves in stir-fries or chop finely and make them into coleslaw. It's a brilliant self-seeder.

Mizuna

An incredibly fast-growing salad green, in summer the leaves are a pickable size just three weeks after sowing. Great for summer as it tolerates warmer conditions. It tolerates cold too. It's just an all-round winner.

Clockwise from top left: Baby spinach leaves; lettuce; mustard greens; kale.

Jack Hobbs, general manager of Auckland Botanic Gardens.

Lettuce as a microgreen

If you are starting lettuces from seed in trays, it's easy to sow
too many, in fact since lettuce seed is tiny I would say it's
impossible not to. But you can eat lettuce and salad green leaves
at basically any stage of growth so don't waste a leaf. Throw
the thinnings into salads or use them like microgreens.
My friend Jack Hobbs from Auckland Botanic Gardens was telling me
that he had sown a tray of different leafy crops, a mix of lettuce, flat-leaf
parsley, cabbage, pak choi and beet. Everything germinated and after
he'd pricked out the seedlings he needed to grow on elsewhere, there was
still plenty left in the tray. So he left the tray in his glasshouse and just
picked leaves from it directly for a few weeks while he was waiting for the
seedlings he had grown on to be established enough to start picking from.
"I just go out there with my scissors," he told me. "Everything in it is
great in a salad and it's a range of colours so it looks great, especially
the beet leaves. And the tray is still growing well and filling out nicely,
thank you very much. And that wasn't even a plan, that just happened."

DIY self-watering planter: Take two plastic buckets or tubs that
will fit one inside the other. Drill several drainage holes in the base
and sides of the inside one, and one or two holes halfway up the
side of the outside one so if the water reservoir gets too full the
water has somewhere to overflow. Add a few decent-sized
stones to the bottom of the outside pot (big enough to make space for the
water reservoir), slot the inside bucket into the outside one, fill and plant.
You can use a regular pot for the inside pot, which will have drainage
holes already, but you do need something that holds water on the outside.

Cut and come again

Cut-and-come-again crops are leafy crops you can harvest from, leaving the roots in the soil to continue to grow, and eventually the edible leaves regrow and you can harvest them again. I love cut-and-come-again crops and grow a lot of them: they are a particularly good choice if you want to produce the maximum food possible in your available space. With a bit of TLC you can easily get a second or third harvest (I find after the third harvest they lose the will to try again and you are better replanting vigorous young seedlings). Try growing leaf lettuces, mizuna, mustard, pak choi, radicchio, kale, rocket, spinach, silverbeet, corn salad and sorrel, as well as leafy herbs like coriander, basil and parsley, in this way. You can harvest all the leaves you have, as on the right, but you can also harvest the outer leaves, one by one, taking just a few leaves at a time, and new leaves will unfurl from the centre of the plant.

_____

Heading brassicas can also produce a second harvest if the roots are left in the ground. With cabbages, broccoli and cauliflower, harvest the mature head leaving as much of the stalk as you can and ideally some outer leaves. You won't get another full-sized head, but you get little mini heads that form around the sides of the stalk. Hearting lettuces have never produced another whole head for me (I know some gardeners who say they sometimes do though), but they will usually produce more edible leaves.

To harvest all the leaves you have, then cut the whole plant off about 3cm above the soil line, leaving the roots undisturbed.

My mate Candy
Harris in Clarkville
grew all the colours
of nasturtium
available last season.
She uses them under
fruit trees as a living
mulch, and grows
them over supports
to shade leafy greens.

Edible flowers in salads

OK, true confession time, I find edible flowers a little annoying in salads. A huge number of flowers are what I refer to as technically edible, as in they can be eaten without harm, but let's just say I wouldn't sit down in front of a movie with a bowl of them. Quite a few taste of nothing much to me, while others are not, to me at least, especially nice when served raw in a salad. I know this is controversial. People love putting edible flowers in salads and far be it from me to say that is mainly because it makes their salads look better on Instagram. But anyway, if you want edible flowers for your Instagram, I mean, your salads: I think the best options are the tiny blue or white flowers of borage, the mildly garlic-tasting flower of garlic chives, the orange petals of marigolds, the slightly peppery-tasting nasturtium flowers (the leaves have a much stronger peppery taste), the flowers on peas or broad beans, or forget-me-nots, violas or pansies. Lots of herbs have edible flowers, including rosemary, basil, lavender, chives, chamomile, thyme, sage and oregano, but they can be strongly flavoured so a little goes a long way.

Weed it and reap You can also use the flowers from quite a few weeds in salads, try the oniony-tasting flowers of onion weed, or the petals of dandelions. Of course, if you are picking flowers for eating, only do so if you are confident in your identification and you know for sure that they have not been sprayed.

DIY wicking beds

Materials A food grade IBC (intermediate bulk container) • Angle grinder • Drill • Irrigation joiner • Silicon • Irrigation pipe • Scoria • Agricultural pipe • PVC pipe • Geotextile fabric (permeable fabric) • Soil

A wicking garden is a raised vege bed held above a water reservoir. The reservoir is filled with water and that water is wicked (or transported by capillary action) up through the soil to the roots of the plants. When I was in Adelaide recently, I visited the garden of *Gardening Australia* presenter Sophie Thomson and she has wicking beds and just loves them. She told me in summer she has to water her in-ground beds every day but with the wicking beds, she could get away with watering just once a week. You can buy readymade wicking systems – Vegepods (see page 226) are wicking beds – but you can also build them yourself. Sophie talked me through how she built hers.

Step one
Cut your IBC in half. You need something like an angle grinder to cut through the plastic tank and the metal cage. The metal edges that are left are very sharp, but once the IBC is in two halves, flip one half upside down, unscrew the metal cage from the plastic then flip again so the smooth uncut metal edge is at the top. Reinsert the lining. A wicking bed needs to sit on a level flat surface.

Step two
Drill a drainage hole. You often see it suggested to put the drainage hole at a point where the layer of soil meets the water reservoir layer, but Sophie says, after building a few, she now puts the drainage hole close to the ground as that lets you drain all the water out of the bed if you need to. Insert an irrigation joiner into the drainage hole and silicon that in place. Attach a length of irrigation pipe to a pipe elbow and then attach it to the joiner. Turn the angle of the elbow up or down to control the water level.

Step three
Add a thin layer of scoria to the base of the IBC, then coil a length of flexible agricultural pipe on top. Connect one end of that to a length of PVC pipe that is attached to the side so it sits above the top of the bed and can be used to fill the reservoir. Cover the ag pipe with more scoria, level it, then cover the scoria layer with geotech fabric (it stops the soil from washing into the scoria-water level and clogging it up). Then add a 20–30cm layer of soil on top. Thoroughly saturate the soil, fill the reservoir and start planting.

Sophie's patch These are Sophie's wicking beds. She puts wooden boards on the outside to insulate the beds and make them look tidier.

Other ways of wicking

Sophie told me, having made a few wicking beds (she has 22 at her place), she has refined her technique. She now uses a commercial wicked bed insert, known as WaterUps (not available in New Zealand), rather than scoria. The difference, she said, is how much water the reservoir can hold: WaterUps hold about 50 percent more water than scoria. Sheryn Dean built the wicking bed in the bottom pics in her Waikato garden: she doesn't use a fabric layer and says it's essential to have the base soil level irregular, going down though the scoria and pipe so the 'wick' is in constant contact with the water and the wicking action continues as the water level drops.

Step-by-step Sheryn Dean, the editor of *OrganicNZ*, built the bottom wicking bed.

I pop herbs everywhere in my vege beds to fill gaps. This bed has parsl dill, rosemary, nasturtium, marjorar and dill tucked in between the plan

Grow herbs everywhere

Herbs should be in every
garden, frankly in every meal.
They look good, taste good
are good for you... really, what
more could you ask of them?

If you grow nothing else, grow herbs. When it comes to bang for buck, you cannot go past them.

use herbs every day, in almost every single thing I cook or eat. In the iconic New Zealand book, *The Cook's Herb Garden*, by sisters Mary Browne, Helen Leach and Nancy Tichborne, which I absolutely love, the authors take issue with the fact that in recipes the word 'optional' is often included in brackets after any herbs are mentioned, and I agree: culinary herbs are as essential to the flavour of the resulting dish – more sometimes – than some of the main ingredients.

I think one of the best things about gardening is growing herbs and being able, when I choose, to add them to everything I cook in generous handfuls rather than the stingy teaspoon and half tablespoon measures that recipes often suggest.

You don't need a separate growing space for herbs, you can also pop them here are there in your vege beds to fill any gaps, as I often do, or grow them among your ornamental plants. Plenty are attractive enough to hold their own, and many are wonderful for bringing in beneficial bugs. You don't need much space either, lots of herbs are fantastically productive in containers. Mainly they are untroubled by pests and pretty easy to grow provided you get the timing right with the tender annual ones.

There are perennial herbs that you plant once and can harvest from for years – rosemary, thyme, mint and bay, for instance These represent fantastic value for any money you spend on the original plant. Then there are plenty of annual herbs, like parsley, coriander and dill, which, under the right conditions, self-seed so reliably you can plant them once and just leave them be. In fact dill self-seeds almost too reliably here and pops up everywhere but the seedlings are easy enough to spot (you'll see two long narrow cotyledon leaves first, but after that the seedlings produce that distinctive feathery foliage).

Lots of herbs are as useful in the garden, as in the kitchen: you can use them as groundcovers or low hedges, or let them cascade over the edges of raised beds or down retaining walls.

Herbs are also fantastic to grow if you are looking to cut your food bill. Not that many offer a meal in themselves, of course, but they cannot be beaten for adding wow factor to meals and a huge punch of flavour to budget-friendly ingredients like dried pulses or beans and cheaper cuts of meat. Honestly, grow all the herbs you can and grow them everywhere. I promise you, your life will be the better for it.

I add finely chopped rosemary (I use the spice-grinding attachment on a food processor) when I make shortbread. Try it, it's delicious.

Clockwise from top left: Basil; bay leaves; try bay as a standard; basil in a pot.

My (arguably) essential herbs

Here are the edible herbs I wouldn't be without in my own garden. But this list is by no means exhaustive. Pick and choose the ones you use, or like the sound of, to grow at your place, and add any extras as you desire.

Basil

I love basil. I love the taste and I love the smell, honestly, I would wear the scent of basil as a perfume if I could (fun fact: the main culinary species of basil's botanical name is *Ocimum basilicum*: ocimum comes from the Greek word for smell and basilicum meaning kingly or royal).

It's easy to grow from seed or seedlings too provided you wait until it's warm enough. Basil is a tropical plant. Even if the days are reliably warm, if the nights are cold it will not do well. You can start the seed inside, on a seedling heatpad if you have one, and plant out when nights are warmer than 10°C but in my Auckland garden, I wait until late October or November and sow direct. I find seedlings that have been cosseted indoors tend to be more fussy and finicky when you eventually plant them outside. But in regions where the summers are shorter, I would start from seed inside or buy seedlings and grow it in a pot. Provided you keep the watering up, basil loves pots: and the soil in pots is always a little warmer than the ground. You can also grow this herb undercover in a tunnelhouse or on a windowsill.

There are lots of different sorts of basil, with quite different flavour profiles. I love the Genovese varieties, 'Sweet Genovese' has what I'd call a classic basil taste and is a good choice if you plan only to grow one or if you've not grown it before. But if a friend has a variety you don't know nibble on a leaf of it, if you like the taste grow that too.

Bay

I was given a bay tree in a pot as a housewarming gift some 15-odd years ago and I still have it, in the same pot, and pick from it often. It was such a good housewarming present, that I took to giving it to anyone I knew who bought a house, including my friends Karolina and Thomas. They planted it in the ground where it grew so well it threatened to overwhelm their outdoor space and I believe they needed to get an arborist in at some expense. So be aware that bay can get tall, easily up to 5 or 6m – in fact, I have read about them reaching 20m eventually (after a good while it is fair to say, they are quite slow-growing). They could not be easier to grow once you have a plant, but they are tricky to propagate. You can try from cuttings (semi-ripe cuttings in late summer or softwood ones in early summer), but I'd either buy a plant from a garden centre or drop some hints next time you buy a house.

Clockwise from top left: Chamomile; chives; both chives and chamomile will grow in a pot.

Chamomile

My friend Yotam Kay from Pakaraka Permaculture in Thames told me a few years ago you can grow chamomile from a chamomile tea bag – which makes sense really, as the tea is made up of dried flower heads and so inevitably includes seed. I found a very aged teabag in the pantry and gave it a go, and several dozen plants germinated. I haven't had to do it again as chamomile is a reliable self-seeder and now pops up here and there.

Fresh chamomile tea tastes quite different to the sort you make with a bought teabag. To make it, just pop the flower heads off the stems until you have about two or three tablespoons and steep in boiling water. I usually put a sprig of mint or spearmint in too. Chamomile tea is famous for its ability to reduce stress and anxiety and help you sleep. Jane Wrigglesworth, author of *The Everyday Herbalist*, who wrote a herb column for *NZ Gardener* for more than a decade and is studying to be a medical herbalist, told me chamomile is an anti-inflammatory too, and great if you struggle with gut inflammation.

The chamomile used in tea is German chamomile, which is a tallish (60cm or so) annual plant. There's also a low-growing perennial chamomile, usually called Roman chamomile, sometimes Russian or English chamomile. That's the chamomile you want if you aim is to grow a chamomile lawn, although go for a non-flowering cultivar or you will get bald patches if you don't deadhead.

Chives

Chives will do very well in the ground but I grow mine in a pot. Like many herbs, they need very good drainage but they also need to stay moist: their wild relatives are found on river banks and in marshes. If chives dry out they tend to be almost immediately infested with little black allium aphids. To stop the pot my chives are growing in drying out too quickly, I usually move it in summer to a spot that offers afternoon shade. If your plant gets infested by aphids, you can squash them with your fingers, hose them off or (the best option) spray them off with a dissolved soap solution. Just dissolve about a teaspoon of dishwashing liquid (use an eco-one that's plant-based rather than a petroleum-derived sort) in a half bucket of water. The fatty acids in the soap disrupt the aphids' cuticle layer, the protective exoskeleton on the outside that protects them from damage and stops water loss, and that kills most of them (but never all of them, in my experience). You need to keep doing it regularly to keep ahead of the aphid population but you can use the same dissolved soap spray to help manage the populations of other small soft-bodied sap-sucking insects like whitefly and thrips.

Common chives are sometimes called onion chives to distinguish them from garlic chives, which are a related but different plant – taller with broader, flatter leaves and producing loose white flowers rather than the purple pompoms of common chives. Remember chives are perennial, so they die back in winter and should reappear in spring.

Grow chives along the edges of vege beds and let them flower freely to bring in the bees. The flowers, both the purple and the white ones, are edible too.

Grow your own spices

You might already be growing coriander, celery, dill, fennel or mustard – just save the seed to stock your spice rack. Less commonly grown are anise, cumin, and caraway, and again you just need to save and dry the seed (I have also heard of cardamom growing in New Zealand, but only undercover). You can also grow your own paprika by growing a paprika pepper (which is a kind of capsicum), drying the fruit and grinding it. One year when I must have been feeling very time-rich I grew the paprika pepper 'Alma' and dried the fruit over smoke on our Weber to make a homegrown smoked paprika. If you are in a region that has a cold winter and a hot dry summer, you can grow the world's most expensive spice, saffron (don't even try it in Auckland or Northland but it's worth a go on the east coast of the South Island; plant saffron corms in a pot, it needs perfect drainage). You can also grow turmeric and ginger – see the instructions on pages 113 and 108 respectively, literally just plant the roots that you buy in the shops. You can grow both inside year-round inland or down south, or if you just don't have much outdoor space. Jane Wrigglesworth told me she grows both ginger and turmeric as houseplants very successfully, and harvests enough for her needs from her indoor plants.

Clockwise from top left: Curry leaf; coriander; dill; in cold places keep curry leaf in a pot.

Coriander

I like to think of coriander as a moody teenager. It takes very little to set it off – a change of temperature, a dry spell, a windy day – and its reaction can be hard to predict, although it is very prone to bolting immediately to seed. It also usually dislikes being transplanted. I have transplanted very small seedlings in jiffy pots successfully, but the plants do form a long tap root and if that is disturbed, they will (spoiler alert) bolt. I wouldn't bother trying to transplant bigger, more mature plants. You are far better to sow this from seed where you want it to grow. I find it tricky to grow all year – in summer, it just bolts for me – but lots of gardeners have told me they manage a year-round supply by sowing a bit of seed every couple of weeks from early spring until early autumn (the autumn-sown plants should keep producing over winter).

It's possible to grow it in pots but choose a bigger pot, as the smaller ones just dry out too fast. Coriander does best in soil that is moist but, as an impossible-to-please teenager, hates having wet feet and if you leave it sitting in water it will (and you might be able to guess this) bolt. But if it does bolt, remember you can harvest the seed for sowing and/or for your spice rack (see page 105) and the airy white flowers are beloved of beneficial insects.

Curry leaf

I love South Indian food, and that often includes curry leaf, which you almost never see in the shops and need to grow yourself. It's used in Sri Lankan dishes a lot too. Curry leaf is in no way related to curry powder; I have seen the flavour described as like citrus, lemongrass, anise and asafoetida. To me it tastes like curry leaf.

Curry leaf is a subtropical plant. I have it outside in my garden but if you get a frost, I'd keep it in a pot undercover (I know someone who grows it as a houseplant in her kitchen). Mine is about a knee-height shrub after a few years, although *NZ Gardener*'s deputy editor Mei Leng Wong (she grows curry leaf in a half wine barrel in her garden in Auckland) says growing up in Malaysia, curry leaf would grow as a tree, well over head height. But she has only once seen it get taller than waist height in New Zealand. Just be aware there's another low-growing plant with grey foliage called curry plant, to which curry leaf is in no way related and it cannot be used in food in the same way (fun fact: curry plant is not used in curry powder either).

Dill

I grow a lot of gherkins, or pickling cucumbers, and my favourite way to preserve them is as dill pickles, which means I need to grow dill as you rarely see it for sale and even when you do, its feathery foliage does not last off the plant.

In the garden treat it a bit like that moody drama queen coriander as, like coriander, it is prone to bolting should conditions be in any way not to its liking. It also forms a taproot and resents being transplanted so sow it in situ. You can keep sowing regularly so that new plants keep coming on although given its propensity for bolting, in the right conditions you can rely on it to self-seed too.

Fennel

Fennel and dill have similar feathery foliage but they are different plants and taste different: fennel has a much stronger aniseedy taste. Also, dill is an annual but the fennel I grow in my gardens is the foliage of the bulbous Florence fennel (technically perennial but if you want to harvest the bulbs, just grow it as annual; you can also grow sweet fennel, which doesn't form a bulb). But Florence fennel and sweet fennel are cultivars of the leafy fennel that grows as a weed all over the country (that weedy fennel doesn't produce a bulb but the leaves and seeds are perfectly edible if they have not been sprayed, I often see people foraging from plants that grow along Sandringham Road in Auckland).

For a plant that is so closely related to a weed, it is, unsurprisingly, easy to grow. But it doesn't like to get too hot and is prone to bolting if it dries out. It doesn't like being transplanted either so sow seed in early spring everywhere and then again in warmer regions from early to mid-autumn.

Ginger

Growing edible ginger is as simple as buying a fresh plump rhizome, with lots of eyes (growth buds) on the surface, from the supermarket or farmer's market, and planting it in spring. It's a tropical plant but I have heard of gardeners growing it as far south as Christchurch (in a pot and inside). Actually, wherever you are, grow it in a pot: it needs perfect drainage, plus it makes it much easier to harvest from. A reader got in touch with *NZ Gardener* years ago to tell us that she grew culinary ginger (along with galangal and turmeric) in just the fine coco coir mulch brick-shaped blocks in a 40L pot, giving it a liquid feed when she remembered. To harvest, she just spread out a plastic tarp, dumped the mix on it, took out as much ginger as she needed and then replanted.

Horseradish

I absolutely love horseradish. I usually process the root in a food processor although be aware it has an extremely pungent odour as it breaks down – think much, much more eye-watering than onions. Open doors and windows before you start; or do what I do and use an extension lead to take the food processor out onto the back deck. It is criminally easy to grow: borderline invasive. Keep it in a decent-sized pot as it will take over any bed or border that it grows in. The foliage dies down in winter, but I all but guarantee it will come back again in spring because at my place it seems unkillable. It also will grow from any piece of the plant so if you want to grow it, just get a piece of root from a friend or a fancy grocer.

Lemongrass

Lemongrass is a clump-forming perennial grass and you use the peeled base crushed or finely chopped in curry pastes. It's another tropical plant: I grow it outside year-round in a pot in my Auckland garden, but in colder places I'd suggest shifting it inside over winter. To propagate, you can divide established clumps with a spade in summer (and you should as otherwise the clumps get congested and less productive).

Clockwise from top left: A (rather spindly) horseradish stem; lemongrass; fennel; ginger.

Clockwise from top left: Lemon verbena; makrut lime leaves; mint; oregano.

Lemon verbena

I love lemons and so have a soft spot for lemon verbena, which has a sweet lemon taste. It's a perennial and evergreen in frost-free areas but will be deciduous in areas with cold winters, and can die altogether in a hard frost. So, either grow it in a pot that you can move inside or treat it as an annual down south. The leaves themselves are quite tough, I find them nicer infused into a tea or a sugar syrup rather than eaten raw (you can also put the leaves in one of those organza bags and throw it into the bath, the smell is amazing). Grow it from cuttings or buy a plant: it doesn't seem to set seed here. Be aware under the right conditions it can grow big, about 3m by 3m. At Auckland Botanic Gardens there is a lemon verbena that I would describe as a small tree.

Jane Wrigglesworth told me if you don't like chamomile's taste, grow lemon verbena and make tea from that, as like chamomile it reduces anxiety and promotes sleep and frankly, to me, it tastes much nicer.

Makrut lime

This is another plant I was given as a housewarming gift 15 years ago, which is still thriving, although unlike the bay tree I have repotted it. Most makrut limes in New Zealand are grafted onto a dwarfing rootstock so they grow well in pots, which you can move inside or into a sheltered spot in colder places over winter (like all citrus they are frost-tender, but you can plant them in the ground in frost-free places). Like all citrus they are greedy feeders, I feed mine a couple of times over the warmer months while the plant is actively growing. You grow makrut limes for the aromatic foliage, which I mainly just use in curry paste although I saw a tip in *Cuisine* magazine years ago to add two leaves to rice before cooking, which I have done ever since.

Marjoram/oregano

These are not the same plant but closely related although purists would point out that the flavour of marjoram (*Origanum majorana*), often called sweet marjoram, is lost if you cook it, so it's better added just before serving or as a garnish, while oregano (*Origanum vulgare* and its many subspecies), also called wild marjoram, is what gives you the much stronger classic oregano flavour. You can grow both of them in a pot or the ground, but be aware that the *Origanum vulgare* species can spread and self-seed freely. It's theoretically possible to grow marjoram and oregano from seed but given the fact that in a home garden you won't need more than a plant or two, just buy a seedling or ask a friend to divide their plant in spring.

Mint

People say mint should be grown in a pot, as it's a thug that takes over, but I love it so let it run rampant in an ornamental border. There are lots of sorts of mint of various minty-ness: if you find one that appeals in a friend's garden, just dig up a piece of rooted stem to plant. You can also divide mint and it will root from a stem in fresh water. To be honest the propagation of mint is much easier than the eradication of mint once it is established. It does best in a moist spot.

If mint gets too dry, it is prone to rust. If it gets rusty though, cut it right back to the ground and water well, and fresh, rust-free foliage should appear.

Parsley

Obviously, everyone should grow parsley. It's not very fussy, fine in a pot and sweet as in the ground too although I have flat-leaf parsley in a pot and curly parsley in the ground and the curly parsley is far more prolific. You can also grow it inside for use in the kitchen. I have seen curly parsley in ornamental gardens and in hanging baskets and it looks great, the strong green colour makes it an excellent plant for filling any gaps. One year at the Melbourne International Flower and Garden Show I even saw curly parsley used as a hedge (it was in a vertical planter that was like a lot of stacked capital Vs so the 'hedge' was made up of horizontal rows of plants, if that makes sense). It looked excellent although using it as a hedge would produce a lot of parsley, you'd have to really like tabbouleh.

Parsley is a biennial, flowering and setting seed in its second year and then dying. The leaves are better in the first year so you can grow it as an annual but I let my plants (both curly and flat) set seed freely and always have fresh plants coming up.

Rosemary

Easy-going rosemary loves pots and does well in the soil. Its flowers are beloved by bees, the prostrate forms make a wonderful groundcover while the upright forms are a useful hedge. It's easy from cuttings too.

Sage

Once you get the conditions right, sage is easy to grow but it's another herb I grow in a pot to give it the good drainage it requires. I have tried it in the soil several times, and killed it. If you have free-draining soil though, grow it in amongst your ornamentals. Common sage holds on to its silvery-green leaves all year and can look very attractive en masse, there's also an edible purple sage where the new leaves start off purple and age to that classic sage colour. I don't like the taste of the leaves raw at all, but cooking changes the flavour altogether. Try flash-frying individual leaves in butter for about 15 seconds and serving them on eggs or gnocchi. You can grow sage from cuttings and layering I am told, but I must admit I have never tried propagating this herb; it's not the sort of herb you use (or at least I use) by the handful so I only need one or two plants on the go which I just pick up, as required, from the garden centre.

Tarragon

If you are growing tarragon, make sure you have the French tarragon, not the closely related Russian tarragon, the flavour of which is nowhere near as good. I grow tarragon in a big pot to keep track of it, as it is a herbaceous perennial so it dies right back in winter, but you can grow it in the ground too – just remember where it is as it's not especially vigorous so can be overwhelmed by other plants. Tarragon has a delicate liquorice flavour, which is nicer than that sounds. You need it to make a classic Béarnaise sauce but my favourite way to use it is chopped up and mixed into butter to serve on steak.

Thyme

Thyme is another herb that is so easy to grow it is literally a weed across much of Central Otago. It doesn't like wet feet and needs good drainage, so once again I grow it in a pot but it does well in the ground too. It's easy to grow from cuttings and you can also divide established plants.

Turmeric

You can grow turmeric like ginger (it's in the same plant family) but it's far more finicky and far, far more frost-tender, and it can be harder to find the fresh rhizomes in the shops to plant. You sometimes see it suggested to let the growing sprouts appear before you plant (like you would chit potatoes) but the late subtropical plantsman

Russell Fransham, from Matapouri, told me just to plant the rhizome shoot end down. Give it rich soil and perfect drainage: wherever you are, grow it in a pot and keep it inside over winter. It dies right back in winter and you will think (or I always think) that you have killed it but it should come back again in summer. Once it is established, you can dig down and break off the fresh roots as you need them. After a few years, Russell told me, you need to dig the whole clump up in spring and divide it or it will get too congested.

Vietnamese mint

Vietnamese mint is a completely different, unrelated plant to mint but also worth growing for the kitchen, I throw it in pho, laksa and Vietnamese-style beef salad. It likes similar conditions to mint and like mint is a super spreader, I grow it in a pot to contain its colonising ways. You can grow a new plant easily from a stem in fresh water, in fact I actually heard from a reader who kept stems in a vase of fresh water for months, topping up the water regularly and harvested it as she needed although she did say a thicket of roots would eventually form in the water and they needed to be fairly regularly trimmed back.

Vietnamese mint is sometimes called Vietnamese coriander or rau ram. I use it interchangeably with coriander and mint, but it is stronger tasting so use less.

To increase the chance of your supermarket herbs surviving, transplant them as soon as possible after you buy them.

Herbs from the supermarket

If you have purchased those very spendy herbs from the supermarket, that are actual plants growing in pots, it is absolutely worth trying to transplant them into your garden after you have used them in whatever you bought them to make. I was talking to Brigitte de Cabissole, from Superb Herb which is a supplier of living herbs to supermarkets, and she said the most common question she gets asked by customers is if the herbs have been treated with something that will stop them from growing after you buy them. "And they haven't been!" she told me. But bear in mind that those living herb plants have been grown under very controlled conditions – for instance, Superb Herb grows their herbs undercover in a semi-hydroponic situation, so the plants grow in a pathogen-free soil medium and the exact nutrients they need are provided in water. Unsurprisingly, the rough and tumble conditions in your garden – where they'll face a range of temperatures and weather, and competition from other plants – can be a shock for them. I wouldn't bother transplanting tender soft-leaved supermarket potted herbs like basil and chervil myself, it would likely be too much for their delicate constitutions. Nor would I try with coriander or dill, which both form a tap root and resent being transplanted at the best of times. But do transplant tougher or woody herbs like bay, marjoram, oregano, rosemary, sage, thyme, mint, Vietnamese mint and horseradish. Chives will also transplant fine; I have even divided a supermarket chive plant into smaller clumps to make more plants and every one survived.

Herbs as a
sugar substitute

Stevia should be grown far more than it is. The leaves of this herb are much, much sweeter than sugar and indeed if you dry the leaves and make a powder it can be used as a zero-calorie, safe-for-diabetics sugar replacement: about 2 or 3 teaspoons gives you the equivalent sweetness of a cup of sugar. The downside is that while it tastes incredibly sweet at first it has a strange and not very pleasant aftertaste. Jane Wrigglesworth told me she doesn't use stevia much in teas or baking because the other flavours are not always strong enough to disguise the less palatable aftertaste (although Jane said she did make a successful lemon curd with stevia once and said it tasted great, although it was pale green). But she always uses stevia powder rather than sugar when she is making chutneys or pickles. "The vinegar is a strong enough taste that there's no aftertaste at all," she said. "Plus the vinegar is itself a preservative, so you don't need the sugar to preserve what you're making."

It's a tender perennial that often will die back in winter in New Zealand. It should come away again in spring but in colder places either grow it in a pot and bring it in over winter or treat it as an annual. It's easy to grow from seed, and also very easy from cuttings. Just plant a stem in a cutting mix or pop it in a glass of fresh water, changing the water every day or so. It should form roots quickly.

To make stevia powder fully dry the leaves, then grind them to a powder in a spice grinder or a coffee grinder.

Spring
is here

Spring is the start of the
gardening year. I always feel
awash with positivity for the
growing season ahead and
full of plans and projects.

Spring can make a gardener of anyone. Nature is in a party mood and everyone's invited.

Poets might love spring and bang on about the golden daffodils and happy blossom. But gardeners find it both a busy and a lean time, in that there is a great deal to do – there's certainly no time to waste writing poems, I find – and not a lot to show for it as very little is ready to eat.

Especially at the very start of the season, you are in what is commonly known as the hungry gap. None of the delights of spring – the early asparagus and fresh, sweet-tasting peas – are yet ready. But you have often gone through all your stored root crops and pumpkins, and only brassicas remain. Nothing against brassicas, of course. But sometimes in early spring, for me, they can have the same appeal as a scratchy woollen jumper on a very cold day.

It's tempting to rush to plant and sow as quickly as you can in a rush to the exciting harvests that lie ahead. But spring, I find, is tricky. There is nothing to be gained by rushing ahead early in the season.

Do not be fooled by the appearance of daffodils. It does not mean that spring planting can begin in earnest. A Welsh study found that daffodils started to bloom when the soil temperature was only 6.4°C, which is much too cold for all but the hardiest edible crops.

Don't be fooled by the calendar either.

When I am talking about spring, I am loosely meaning September, October and November. But September in my garden is likely different – quite possibly vastly different – to September in your garden.

The vernal equinox near the end of September, when the days start to become longer than the nights, which is the astronomical start of spring, is a more useful guide but even then, be guided more by the conditions in your garden rather than the date on the calendar.

If you have a soil thermometer, use it: it's the very best way to know if your soil is warm enough for planting. Nothing will produce as well if it started its life under less-than-optimal conditions and the crops that you sow and plant a little later will soon catch up and overtake any you started under marginal conditions.

If you don't have a soil thermometer then the late Prof Walker, the soil scientist who was a host on *Maggie's Garden Show* back in the day, used to recommend going out into the garden and dropping your trousers then sitting your bare bum on the soil. If it was too cold to sit comfortably, then it was too cold to start any heat-loving crops.

I mean you could also buy a soil thermometer; they really are not expensive. But you do you, my friend.

Fragrant white daffodil 'Thalia' in my mate Rachel Clare's garden in Henderson, Auckland. She is a previous deputy editor of *NZ Gardener* and a previous editor of *OrganicNZ*.

Clockwise from top left: Peas in the garden; an heirloom marrow fat pea; garden peas aka shelling peas; climbing peas will need support.

Peas

Peas are simply a delight to grow, and beyond delicious to eat fresh out of the pod. You can cook with them too, of course, but I must admit most of mine are eaten as I pick them. The seeds are easy to handle, and they germinate reliably in cold soil, although I should warn you that everything finds the seed delicious and if you sow direct and the seedlings don't appear it's likely that the seed was eaten by birds, rats or mice. If that happens, start in trays for transplant when the seedlings are about 5cm high (by that stage, a lot of the nutrition in the seed has been exhausted so no-one is as interested in eating it) or protect newly sown seed with a physical cover like a plastic bottle cloche.

Peas like it coolish. In my Auckland garden, I treat them as a shoulder season crop starting in autumn and maybe sowing or planting more in late winter for an extended spring harvest. Down south you can plant or sow in August or September and keep them growing over summer, but I find it gets too humid for them as soon as summer arrives up north and they are struck by powdery mildew before Christmas.

As with beans and tomatoes (and lots of other crops, actually) peas are either determinate (aka bush or dwarf) or indeterminate (aka climbing). There are pros and cons to both: determinate peas produce all their pods basically at once but usually get to about 60 or 70cm; and while they appreciate some support you can get away with planting them in blocks rather than rows and they will support each other (a lovely metaphor for life). I rate the highly productive 'Greenfeast'. Indeterminate peas need about 2m of vertical climbing space, such as a tepee or a trellis, but they keep producing over a longer period and so are far more productive overall. Try the prolific dark-green podded 'Alderman Tall Climbing'.

As well as what I call regular peas (also called shelling peas or garden peas) where you take the peas out of the pods, you can grow mangetout, or snow peas, which you pick before the pods swell and eat whole, and sugar snap peas, which you also eat whole, but the pods are round rather than flat. They are all easy, productive and delicious at every stage. You can also use extra pea seedlings or the leafy tops as microgreens or in salads and the flowers are edible too.

Kids love eating fresh peas. I know someone who told her children that fresh peas were green smarties and, as far as I know, they haven't worked out she's lying yet.

Broad Beans

Broad beans, like peas, are a leguminous crop, and tend to suit the same conditions. In my garden I plant or sow them between mid-autumn and mid-winter to eat over late winter and spring; down south get them in by mid-autumn or wait until early spring. Again, the seed is very easy to handle and easy to sow direct: birds do scratch it up and eat it a bit but not as much as peas, I find.

Most broad beans get to about 1m tall and appreciate a bit of support – tie them on to a trellis or a frame or plant a double row, as in two rows, 30cm apart, leaving about 60cm between each double row with stakes at either end and tie something soft and stretchy about the outside of the whole double row. I rate 'Superaguadulce', 'Coles Prolific' or 'Exhibition Long Pod'. There are also dwarf varieties which you can get away without staking, try 'Coles Early Dwarf' or 'The Sutton' (both of which are good choices for pots and/or windy spots).

Broad beans mainly have black and white flowers but there is a lovely New Zealand selection called 'Hughey' (it's named after the Tapanui plantsman Denis Hughes), which has dark red flowers and looks great in the garden. You can also sometimes get a red-seeded broad bean variety (if you do, save seed, as I had it and lost it and have found it hard to replace) and there's also a new pink-seeded broad bean called 'Lucifer'.

Broad beans are highly prolific but be aware that once they start flowering and setting beans they need access to water; if they dry out, production will slow down or stop. You need to keep picking them regularly to keep beans being produced too.

Broad beans can be harvested and eaten at any stage, really. The tiny, immature pods can be eaten raw in salads or throw them in stir-fries, while mature beans need to be cooked. I like to double-pod them or remove the grey-ish outer skin and only eat the bright green inner bean inside, but you don't have to do that, and if I pick the beans immature (when the beans are no bigger than a pea) then I don't bother. You can also eat the young broad beans shoots in salads.

Broad beans, again like peas, are a nitrogen fixer that you can also use as a green crop (see page 42). Like all leguminous crops, these plants have a symbiotic relationship with rhizobia bacteria, which attach to their roots and convert the nitrogen that's in the air or in the soil into a form that the plants can take up. The plants store the nitrogen in nodes around their roots to use themselves as they flower and fruit – so if you grew broad beans and harvested an edible crop, they won't leave much nitrogen in the soil for what you grow there next. But if you grow them as a cover crop, and chop and drop as they are starting to flower, the nitrogen in the nodes is left in a bioavailable form in the soil for what you grow next.

Broad beans often seem to flower for ages with no beans appearing. Don't stress, they'll come. They only begin to produce viable pollen when it warms up, and often after they start flowering.

Clockwise from top left: Broad beans seedlings; plants in flower; harvest; tie up for support.

Asparagus wrapped in bacon.

Smoosh-ed broad beans: two ways

I love broad beans and my favourite spring breakfast is to blanch a handful or two of broad beans for about three minutes then drain and run under cold water until they are cool enough to handle. Then double-pod the beans (or don't, the outer skins are tougher than the tender inner bean but they are perfectly edible) and mash the beans together with grated parmesan or feta, lemon zest and juice, a splash of olive oil, salt and pepper. Sometimes I throw a bit of garlic in too. I like to serve this on toast with a poached egg on top, but you can also use it as a dip.

A reader also shared a method for using up the old pods, if you skip harvesting for a few days and they mature beyond the young and tender phase, to make a kind of broad bean pate. Blanch and double-pod, as above, then mash with an equal volume of cream cheese. Season with salt, pepper and lemon juice to taste. You can add chopped herbs, crushed capers or diced gherkins too if you have them to hand.

Asparagus wrapped in bacon
(for special occasions only)

My partner Conrad loves bacon and is always suggesting we eat it. But, out of concern for his heart health, I have instituted a rule that it is a special occasion-only food. You can serve these on non-special occasions, but don't tell Conrad. They are super easy to make, just break any woody ends off your asparagus spears, then lay the spears in a flat oven dish with a splash of olive oil and shake them around until they are all a bit oily. I use streaky bacon and cut each rasher in half lengthways with scissors, then wrap a half-rasher around each spear, candy cane-stripe style. Then I bake in the oven dish at 200°C for about 10 minutes on each side. Finally, I usually finish them by putting them straight under the grill for a minute or two. You don't have to, but it makes the bacon much crispier. You can also wrap the asparagus with prosciutto, or in spirals of puff pastry if you want something vegetarian, although it will need a longer cooking time.

Asparagus plants are dioecious, which means there are male and female plants. You often hear you should pull females out: because the girls use up energy producing bright red berries, so the boys are more productive. Indeed there are modern hybrids that produce only male plants. But Matthew Falloon from Aspara Pacific, an asparagus crown and seed producer in Canterbury, says producing all-male hybrids often comes at the cost of disease-resistance. You are better choosing a variety suitable for your conditions, he says: mixed-sex hybrids can and do outperform all-male hybrids in some places. He suggests leaving female plants in situ too: they produce fewer spears but of higher quality, plus trying to dig them out is very likely to damage the vast root structure of the other plants.

Asparagus

Asparagus is more of a long-term marriage than a holiday fling: far more rewarding over the years, of course, but it's more about the steady satisfaction than the immediate gratification, perhaps, and there's probably more work involved. But this perennial crop can be productive for 20 years or more, so all the effort you put in definitely pays off. Again, much like in a marriage.

You can grow asparagus from seed, but most people don't, they buy one-year-old dormant crowns. Even then it's three years before your asparagus plants are really producing much. If you start from seed, it adds a whole extra year to that process.

The crowns are for sale at garden centres in winter and you would think that was because that is the best time to plant them. But actually, you are better to plant them in spring when the soil has warmed up, the (expensive) crowns can rot in very cold soil. So buy the crowns as soon as you see them (they often sell out) and store them in damp potting mix until September or even October in the South Island. This crop needs a permanent situation in the vegetable garden: ideally somewhere a little out of your eyeline as I find the ferny, feathery foliage stage over summer to be a bit weedy looking.

It's worth growing it in a raised bed, even if the rest of your garden is in the ground, as you can better keep on top of the weeds and add sand to improve drainage if necessary. And add any organic matter you have handy to the soil before you plant: compost, seaweed, sheep pellets, an organic source of potash and/or organic fertiliser.

If you have a pH meter (see page 37), it's worth testing your soil before you plant too. Asparagus like a soil pH of between 6.0 and 6.8 – add lime if your soil is acidic. Plant your crowns about 40 or 50cm apart with about 1m between the rows.

Plant the crowns and let them grow and harvest nothing for the first year. Let the spears open up and the feathery foliage form and don't cut it back until it begins to yellow off at the start of winter. In the second year, if the plants are growing well and the spears are at least 15mm in diameter, you can pick a few but don't pick for more than 10 days. In the following year, you can pick for three to five weeks. In the next year, for six to eight weeks. And then in the following year and from then on, you can harvest for between eight and ten weeks, but as soon as the spears get thinner than 10mm in diameter, stop harvesting. Always leave the feathery foliage over the summer until it yellows or browns in winter; don't cut it back early or pick bits of it for floral arrangements. The plant needs every bit of it to feed the underground crowns. The underground crowns themselves are very hardy, but if you get late spring frosts the above-ground spears will get frosted.

The asparagus variety Aspara Pacific's Matthew Falloon recommends for New Zealand vege growers is pythophthora-resistent 'Pacific Challenger', bred by his father, Dr Peter Falloon.

Clockwise from top left: Asparagus foliage; spears; harvest; cut with a knife at ground level.

You can grow potatoes lots of ways. They are a great crop in pots or grow bags, or you can start a single spud in a bucket you have put a few drainage holes in (see page 241). You can grow them in the ground, of course, just dig a trench that's about 15cm deep with the spuds about 30cm apart (earlies) or 45cm apart (main crop) and backfill. Then you can either wait for the leafy tops to be above the soil and cover them with soil again, which is called mounding up, or do as I do and pile extra soil up in a decent mound at the time of planting. It seems to work just as well.

Potatoes

I absolutely love potatoes, and if you don't, we will never be friends. Plant them as soon as the risk of frosts have passed (the leafy tops above ground will go black and die off if they get frosted; I have found the underground tubers will send up more foliage after that happens, but it undoubtedly makes them less productive). Gardeners in the winterless north have told me they start them in early August or July or grow them year-round, but I think you'll get the best yield for the space they take up by waiting for the soil to warm up. I wait until late August in Auckland, and in the South Island I'd hold off until September.

The one argument for planting earlier is you can harvest quick-growing earlies sooner, and that means you'll have them out of the ground well before there's any tomato potato psyllids about. So if you have ongoing psyllid issues, try early planting undercover and/or in containers (see page 254) or try nicotiana planted nearby (see page 23).

Whether you chit, or pre-sprout, early potatoes is up to you. I don't always bother, but it does seem to speed things up once you planted and since you chit them inside before it is warm enough to plant them, it is probably worth doing in colder regions for extra early spuds. To do it, lay seed spuds on newspaper or stand them up in an egg carton out of direct sunlight and wait for the sprouts to reach 10-20mm then plant.

Waxy early spuds are fast-growing but don't store. 'Rocket' and 'Swift' are ready 70-100 days after planting: both do well in pots for me. 'Jersey Benne' does well in the South Island but when my mate, a previous *NZ Gardener* editor, Lynda Hallinan, did early potato trials in her garden in Hunua, 'Jersey Benne' was the poorest performer producing a 6.6kg harvest from 1kg of seed spuds (the best-performer was 'Liseta' which produced 19.6kg from 1kg of seed).

You can plant starchy main-crop potatoes later, from October through to February or March depending on region. But you can also plant at the same time as earlies if you have space. Main-crop spuds take longer, up to 20 weeks, but again planting early means you can harvest them before peak psyllid season. 'Agria' is great, but 'Heather' and 'Rua' both taste wonderful, while New Zealand-bred 'Summer Delight' and 'Summer Beauty' are also delicious and have fantastic disease resistance.

I often make a no-dig potato bed by leaving a straw bale in the weather for a while, then pushing spuds in the sides. Or lay spuds on a clear patch of earth or on cardboard, mulch with about 15cm of straw, throw grass clippings on to stop the straw blowing away and water. You get a higher yield in soil – considerably higher to be honest, but planting in straw makes for super easy harvesting of perfectly clean spuds.

To ensure you have new potatoes on Christmas day, you want to have potatoes chitting by late August and in the ground by mid-September.

Māori potatoes

Definitely try Māori potatoes or taewa. You can plant them at the same time as potatoes, they take up less room and you can't often find them for sale even at farmers' markets and fancy foodie shops, although you certainly see them more than you used to. Taewa (some iwi have other names for them, they are known as mahetau in the south, para-reka on East Coast and peruperu up north) are usually small and knobbly, with dark skin and yellow flesh. I grow these in a pile of organic matter, like potatoes, and they do brilliantly. After 12 weeks I just start digging around and take as many as I need for a meal, you can also leave in the ground for longer (about 16-20 weeks) if you want them to store. My friend Dr Nick Roskruge, a professor of ethnobotany at Massey University and the chair of Tāhuri Whenua, the National Māori Vegetable Growers Collective, told me never to peel them, just wash them, then boil or bake them. They are just delicious with a more buttery taste than the potatoes that were introduced post-European settlement.

Globe artichokes

You can grow artichokes from seed but seriously, I never bother; it takes simply ages. Buy a few plants from the garden centre and plant them in spring and once they get established then they should send up offsets, or pups, at the base that you can cleave off and plant elsewhere. They are short-lived perennials and die right away in winter, and in fact in my clay soil they often die away altogether, although with better drainage they should come back for a few years. In the first spring after planting, you might get just a couple of the edible buds, but from the second year onwards you should get six or eight from each plant. You can eat the buds (see page 134) but you can also leave them to flower: the thistle-like purple flowers make a simply spectacular garden display. Sometimes I even pick them like a cut flower, although they are always covered in bees, so I try not to do that often.

Radishes

Easygoing radishes can be sown almost year-round across much of New Zealand but they do the best in the cool conditions of spring for me and help give you something to harvest when not much is ready. Plus, I think they are sweeter and crisper as a shoulder season crop: if you grow them over hot summers, they taste much hotter. Sow direct and space about 5cm apart. The leafy tops are edible too and can be added to salad or steamed and served like spinach.

Taewa seed spuds are in garden centres in late winter. Don't plant until spring or early summer but buy when you see them, as there's a taewa resurgence going on and the seed spuds sell out.

Clockwise from top left: Globe artichokes; taewa harvest; radishes; the taewa 'Waiporoporo'.

Artichokes a la Nicky's dad

I was always a tad frightened of eating artichokes, but my friend Nicky Pellegrino has an Italian father and served them often when we were round there for dinner. So, after eating them at her place several times I asked how she prepared them, and she shared this method, which she got from her dad Dino.

First clean out any insects living in the artichokes. Do not skip this step.

Then cut off the stem, stuff leaves with a bit of chopped garlic and Italian parsley and place in a lidded pan with enough water to steam – Nicky says start with just a finger-depth or so, you can always add more – and a decent slosh of olive oil, salt and ground pepper. Simmer with lid on until the outside leaves are tender. It takes about 45 minutes depending on size.

At that stage the water will have reduced to a delicious oily juice, and you pour that over the artichoke to serve. Then you pull off the leaves, one by one, dip them in the oil and eat the soft edible end bit of each leaf. When you get to right to the centre there's a hairy layer, called the choke, which is not itself edible. But pull the choke off and the grey/green disc underneath, which is the heart, is edible and entirely delicious.

Heidi's buttered radishes

Radishes are ridiculously easy to grow, and frankly I think that has led to some gardeners not respecting them. I remember, probably a decade ago, I got a long piece of correspondence from an *NZ Gardener* reader called Heidi who labelled radishes "pointless" and "the most un-versatile vegetable ever".

"What are radishes good for?" she wrote to me at the time. "Salad, you'll tell me, they are great in salad. That's the problem. That's all they are good for. And have you ever heard someone say 'all this salad needs is a radish'? Have you ever looked in the fridge and said 'if only I had a radish'?"

After getting Heidi's email, for several weeks I made it a personal quest to ask everyone I met if they ate radishes and if so, how they prepared them. This method, which the French baker round the corner told me about, is the best one I have come across. In my home it is known as Heidi's Buttered Radishes, since she is the reason I found out about it.

Clean your radishes, cut the leafy tops off and cut them in half. Spread the cut half thickly with real butter. Go for the fancy Lewis Road one with salt crystals in if you feel spendy, but otherwise sprinkle a pinch of salt on each half or serve with a dish of flaky salt to dip the buttered side in. You can also slice the radishes, butter them, and serve them on good bread with salt sprinkled over.

'Daikon' are giant white radishes. Use in kimchi or grate and use them like potatoes to make hash browns, Sometimes called tillage radishes: you can use them to break in new ground too.

Heidi's buttered radishes.

Jamie Tucker runs the CSA (Community Supported Agriculture) Laughing Pūkeko Organics in Lincoln. She uses BHU mesh, as well as microclima and reused vineyard bird nets, both to protect crops and raise soil temperature.

Pre-warming soil

I am a big fan of warming up the soil in spring before I plant or sow anything, using cloches or a plastic sheet. You can use a sheet of black or clear polythene that's stretched out in direct contact with the soil, either pegged down or weighted with something like bricks around the edges (if you are buying plastic to do this, get the thickest kind you can so you can use it for several years); or do the same with horticultural fleece. But even a polythene row tunnel, left in place for a few weeks, makes a difference. If the soil temperature is marginal for what you plan to plant, and you can't be bothered trying to warm the soil, plant in raised beds or pots, the soil is always warmer. An *NZ Gardener* reader got in touch with me just the other day to say her brother-in-law couldn't understand why the veges in her 600mm raised bed were growing so much quicker than his in the ground. So, they each tested the soil temperature in their gardens and her soil was a whole 7°C warmer.

You can also use a row tunnel covered with the mesh crop cover fabric sold by the Biological Husbandry Unit at Lincoln University, rather than polythene, to warm up soil. It doesn't increase temperature by a great deal, but research at the BHU found an increase under mesh of 3°C in the maximum temperature and 1°C of the average temperature. Plus the BHU has also shown the insect mesh to be a complete and organic control measure for tomato potato psyllid (TPP) so you can use the same cover to protect your spuds from TPP later in the season.

Summer harvests. Tomatoes ripen off the vine, I often pick while fairly unripe and ripen on my kitchen table to save them from birds.

Summer
at last

Everyone loves summer but
keep on top of watering as
everything in the garden can
quickly get heat stressed
– including the gardener!

Summer comes and everything in the garden goes, or rather grows, into double time.

You need to be everywhere, picking and planting, weeding and watering. And watering and watering. I know it seems basic, but you'd be amazed how many problems that under-watering, over-watering and even irregular watering causes, especially over summer.

Forgive me for stating the obvious but plants need water. Water is as vital to plants as it is to you and me. And gardeners think watering successfully is all about the action of watering, as in how and when you apply water. But actually, it all comes back to the soil (spoiler alert: in gardening, it always comes back to the soil).

Because when you water a plant, you are applying water to the soil in the fond hope that your vegetable crops will get the benefit.

But good soil is both a sieve and a sponge. A sieve in that water needs to be able to move through it. If soil stays saturated, then all the pores – those spaces between the mineral particles and organic matter that make up soil – fill up with water and there is no oxygen available to diffuse into the roots. Your plants will effectively drown.

But you also need soil to be a sponge, as in to hold water around the roots so the plants can take it up as they need it. With large pores (or macropores, which have a diameter of more than 0.08mm), water moves easily

through them and drains away. But smaller pores (or micropores, which have a diameter of less than 0.08mm) are small enough that surface tension holds the water in place. But with very small pores, like you find in very fine silty soil, the water can be held so tightly to the particle surfaces that the force of osmosis in the plants' roots is not strong enough to pull it up. So even though the soil is holding onto any water you apply, it is still not available to your growing crops.

So, watering is not only about how much water you apply but about how much water your soil is able to hold around a plant's roots that it is available to your plants. That water is called plant available water, or PAW. The PAW in a loamy soil can be three times as high as a sandy soil after both soils have been wet to the same degree. And the easiest and quickest way to increase the PAW in your soil is by adding organic matter.

Organic matter in soil – whether that's compost you have applied, winter green crops you have chopped and dropped, or any other soil amendment you have applied that was once alive and is now in a process of decomposition, basically – acts like a sponge. It absorbs and holds water – indeed some types of soil organic matter can absorb up to 20 times their own weight in water – and that water is released slowly as plants need it.

Sunflowers at Sanctuary Gardens Mahi Whenua, a community garden and food forest that is across the road from my house.

Olla pots in situ.
There's also a
terracotta saucer
that sits over the top.

Watering

In my raised gardens I use olla pots, unglazed terracotta pots with a narrow neck and a round fat bottom, which are a cheat's way to increase soil's water-holding capacity. You bury them up to the neck in the soil and fill them with water, which seeps through the pores of the permeable terracotta and is sucked into the dry soil. I like them because they deliver water directly to the plant root zone where it is useful.

They also deliver water slowly. I know the temptation to rush around with the hose set to a waterblaster jet level, but no good comes of applying water faster than soil can absorb it. If you do, it can cause run-off, where the water skims across the surface of where you are applying it and moves downhill; and leaching – when water carries dissolved soil, or pesticide or fertiliser, with it as it moves downs through the pores in the soil.

The thing that's worth remembering in summer, is it's not about watering more, it's about watering more efficiently, more smartly and frankly more responsibly. Apply water slowly and gently at soil level so it soaks into the soil rather than runs off the top. Use mulches and temporary shade to reduce the amount of water lost through evaporation. Increase the organic matter in soil to help it hold on to the water available. And keep on top of your weeding. Every weed is competing for resources, including water, with what you want to grow.

And if your veges are failing to thrive and you just can't work out all why, consider investing in a soil moisture meter. You can buy them at any box store or hardware store, they are not very expensive. And then you will know for sure that the moisture level in your soil suits the edible crops you are growing, and if it doesn't you can refine your watering techniques. It's amazing how many problems you can solve simply by providing consistent, adequate access to water.

The only downside I have found to olla pots is in autumn and winter, when I am not filling them, they become Airbnbs for slugs and snails who appreciate any dark, moist hiding spot where they can rest during the day.

Tomatoes

I absolutely love tomatoes. I love growing them. I love eating them fresh and I love cooking with them. Homegrown tomatoes are easy, prolific and delicious, and while many crops are one or even two of those things, few are as reliably all three.

They are easy from seed. Dangerously easy in fact, one year I accidentally grew 342 of them – I had seedlings everywhere, the spare room, the kitchen table, the rear parcel tray of my car (if you don't have space to start seedlings, a parked car makes a surprisingly effective greenhouse, on a sunny day the temperature inside a parked car can be twice what it is outside).

You absolutely should not grow 342 tomatoes. It's ridiculous to do so, given what you can produce off one well-maintained plant. I don't keep records every year of what I harvest from my garden but one year I was involved in a tomato-growing competition with some of my colleagues (which I won, just saying). I weighed most of the tomatoes I picked from my competition plants that year and there was easily more than 50kg from just five bush plants without doing anything special (if it had been vine tomatoes, it probably would have been more).

What sort to grow?

There are so many amazing and interesting tomato varieties out there, especially if you start them from seed, and I see the temptation to try and grow all of them, or at least 342 of them, I really do. But honestly, after many years of gardening I increasingly think you are better off in the home garden growing fewer plants, giving them more space (good airflow is vital for tomatoes) and giving more time to the plants you have (see page 20).

Tomatoes are either determinate (bush) or indeterminate (vine). It should be written on the seed packet, or the plant label if you are buying seedlings. I grow both sorts. Determinate tomatoes are shorter, not much more than 1m. You don't really need to take the laterals off (see page 182) and while they appreciate some support, you can get away

If you live in a region where heat-loving summer crops like tomatoes and eggplants are marginal (especially tricky eggplants), then small-fruited varieties (like cherry or medium-sized tomatoes or the smaller egg-shaped or sausage-shaped eggplants) give you a better chance at a good yield. Or try grafted tomato or eggplant seedlings, which are both more prolific and quicker to produce.

My tomatoes. I left too many laterals on last season, and at this point of the season they had turned into an absolute thicket.

Clockwise from top left: This is the year I grew 342 seedlings; planting; if you have problems with psyllid, try a neem oil-based spray; stake at planting and keep tying the stem on with something soft.

without staking them. If you do stake them, you only need to stake them to a metre or so. Indeterminate tomatoes easily top 2m in height and need a stake of an equivalent height. Determinate toms produce all their flowers at once and all the fruit on the plant is ready over a week or two (which is quite good if you are preserving as you have a decent harvest to make into relish or sauce at one time). Indeterminate tomatoes will continue flowering and fruiting throughout the growing season, so are a better choice when you want a steady supply of tomatoes.

Tomatoes are also classed as early, middle or late depending on how soon after planting you can expect fruit. I try to plant a mix to extend my tomato harvest season: the earlies fruit in about 70 days, the mid-season about 80 or 90, and the lates more than 90 days. In regions with short summers focus on the mids and the early varieties.

I have seen again and again how differently the same tomato variety performs in different parts of the country, which offer different growing environments. I mean that's true for all vegetables, but particularly true for tomatoes. So, don't be guided by my suggestions, ask gardeners living around you what performs best for them. But in my Auckland garden, I always grow 'Black Krim' because I love the flavour and it deals well with humidity, and the determinate heirloom 'Scoresby', which has lovely and succulent fruit perfect for sandwiches and preserving. I used to grow 'Moneymaker' but I was interested to see it wasn't particularly productive in tomato trials held at the Auckland Botanic Gardens a few years ago, and since then I have grown 'Early Money', which was one of the most productive in those trials. I always put in a 'Sweet 100', which are absolute workhorses producing sweet cherry tomatoes in incredible abundance ('Black Cherry' is a good choice if you like tarter cherry tomatoes). Every year I try one new tomato variety that I have not grown before, and by one I mean up to three.

Sowing and planting

With tomatoes I am growing from seed, I start seed in propagation trays inside my house (or car) in early spring, usually September, and grow them on inside so I have decent-sized plants to plant outside late October or November (in Auckland I sometimes sow more from seed in December and add a second round of plants in January to extend the harvest, but only do that in regions where you anticipate at least another three months of warm weather). You can start them earlier inside, lots of people start them in late winter, even midwinter, but frankly I think you can sow tomato seed too early. You don't want to be fussing about with seedlings inside for months and months while you wait for it to be warm

How to freeze tomatoes. If you cannot be bothered labouring over a hot preserving pan when everyone you know is at the beach, you can freeze excess tomatoes whole. Just chop out the stem and place in a single layer in a freezer tray, then when frozen transfer to freezer bags. The texture of tomatoes turns mushy after they have been frozen but you can use them in any recipe that calls for canned tomatoes over the year.

enough to shift them outside. Inevitably, even with constant care and attention, the seedlings get leggy and stretched.

I start the tomato seed in trays on a heatpad. They appreciate heat from below: try them on the floor of your bathroom if you have underfloor heating. But if you have neither a seedling heatpad nor underfloor heating, don't stress. You can also cover your trays with something like a resealable plastic bag and seal it to make a mini hothouse (remove it as soon as seedlings appear). They need heat but not light to germinate, so you can pop them anywhere warm, like the top of the fridge or even in the hot water cupboard, just take the tray out into the light as soon as seedlings appear.

Planting on Labour weekend is all very well, but tomatoes are absolute heat lovers so hold off if the night temperatures are still cool. You can plant in November or even December, so wait if you think conditions are less than ideal. When I grew up in Christchurch, we never shifted our tomatoes into the garden until Canterbury show weekend, which was late November. Now in my Auckland garden I like to wait until the point in the year when, if we are sitting outside after dinner, I don't need to go inside and get a hoodie. They would survive if I planted them sooner than that, I know lots of Auckland gardeners have them in much earlier. But I find they don't produce as well over the whole season and with limited space in my garden, I want to get the maximum yield from the space they take up.

When you are planting tomatoes bury them deeply, so the soil line is right below the first set of leaves. Tomatoes, especially heirloom tomatoes, produce adventitious or aerial roots along the stem (if you look closely, you can see them, like little bumps or hairs). In contact with the soil, these grow into normal roots so planting deeply helps the plant develop a larger, stronger root system, which will mean a healthier, stronger and more productive plant.

Spacing, staking and soil

I usually prepare the soil where I plan to grow them with organic blood and bone and dolomite lime, maybe a little organic sulphate of potash. Throw on a decent layer of compost too. Leave at least 50cm between the plants, probably more like 80 or 90cm if you are prone to being lazy about taking the laterals off and tying the stem to the stake, and instead let them sprawl all over the ground. Good airflow and not overcrowding tomato plants prevents many of the potential problems that tomatoes are prone to.

Stake them or otherwise support tomatoes at the time of planting, especially indeterminate varieties. It seems ridiculous putting a 2m stake next to a tiny seedling, but you will regret it later if you don't. I have tried those readymade tomato cages and don't like them for indeterminate tomatoes, they make it harder to get to the plant to

You can also plant tomatoes sideways, as in dig a trench and lay the tomato in it, then burying the stem up to the first leaves. Don't worry that the tomato starts out laying down, it quickly turns itself upright again.

Clockwise from top left: A tomato cage of bamboo stakes; training up strings; a lateral; Garry Foster in the Wairarapa adds bottles to the top of the tomato stakes, that way he can throw nets over the top.

Garry Foster uses physical barriers extensively to protect crops at Matahiwi Forest Garden in Wairarapa.

take the laterals off and the growth ends up congested inside the cage (they are OK for determinate tomatoes I suppose, but I now use them to support my dahlias).

If you are growing tomatoes on individual stakes, you want to grow your tomatoes as a single leader, which is a single long tomato vine, or I often do a double leader where you let two leaders develop and tie one to each side of the stake. Tomatoes naturally want to sprawl about the place making as many stems as possible, so to support them on a single stake you need to delateral them or take off the side shoots that form at the axis of the main vine and the side branches, which want to become stems too. Check the plant every couple of days, laterals form incredibly quickly.

You can just pinch the laterals off between your fingers if you catch them quickly enough, but if you let them get too big before you catch them, use your snips. Keep tying the main stem onto the stake too with something soft and stretchy.

You can also grow tomatoes against a trellis or some other kind of vertical support, either as a row of single leader tomatoes or a couple of plants supporting multiple stems like a fan espalier. Or you can string train them like the commercial growers do. String training is especially good if you are growing them in a tunnelhouse or undercover as that means you probably have an overhead beam or something like that to hang the string off.

You can grow tomatoes in pots too (see page 254), but pots do dry out quickly so be prepared to water every day or two. Tomatoes in the ground you need to water at least twice a week, more often when it's hot and/or dry. Consistent watering is absolutely key to a successful tomato harvest. If their access to water is irregular, the fruit will split or develop sunken black patches at the base, which is known as blossom end rot.

Once my tomatoes start flowering, I start feeding them with a dilute liquid tomato fertiliser (often at a higher dilution rate than recommended on the bottle, aka the weakly-weekly approach, see page 249) every couple of weeks. You can cut off the lower leaves if they start to yellow off or even if they don't it still improves airflow around the plant.

It's fair to say tomatoes are prone to all sorts of pest problems, and the best and most effective control method I have seen is growing them under a physical cover made of the insect mesh from the Biological Husbandry Unit at Lincoln University (see page 137).

It's easier to use with low-growing plants like potatoes where you can just throw it over hoops – tall upright plants like tomatoes require you to rig up some kind of tent-like structure – but physical barriers are an extremely effective way to prevent many pest problems, plus tomatoes appreciate the microclimate created by the mesh crop cover.

When you take laterals off, pop them into a glass of water so the bottom end is submerged. Roots will form and you can plant them. You don't even have to do that to be honest, you can just push them straight int soil and they usually grow. But I am warning you, if you try and save every lateral you will end up with far, far too many tomato plants.

Tomato salsa

I love this recipe. It came from a *NZ Gardener* reader years ago. I make as much as I can every year, as it's so easy and we burn thought it. I must admit though, some of my friends and family are a little cautious around my salsa. Not that it's not delicious – it is, so much better than the bought stuff – but because I never remember to record what sort of chilli I have used. And I grow a lot of different sorts of chillies (see page 164), including some that are fairly mild and some that are extraordinarily hot. I don't mind – I love hot chilli – but if you are not a fan, it's fair to say that salsa is something of a Russian roulette at my place.

To make it, chop 1.5kg tomatoes, 3 onions, 7 cloves of garlic and add it all to a pot with 3-6 teaspoons of minced chilli, 1 cup of white vinegar and 1 teaspoon of salt. Cook until reduced (45 minutes or so), then add 3 chopped capsicums, cook until they're soft, pour into hot sterilised jars and seal. This recipe scales up no problem, when my tomatoes are in full production I often make a double or a triple batch.

No-cook pasta sauce

This is so simple but so delicious provided – and I cannot stress this enough – you have ripe, sweet tomatoes. It's even better when they are fractionally over-ripe. Don't try and make it with bought tomatoes out of season, you deserve better than that. Just chop up a few tomatoes (if I am making this just for myself I usually use three or four bigger tomatoes), a couple of cloves of garlic and a good handful of basil. Add salt, pepper and a dash of olive oil or a spoonful of butter (don't worry about melting it, the hot pasta does that). Sometimes I throw a diced chilli in too or the juice of a lemon. If I am swamped by zucchini, I grate one and throw that in. Mix it all up and leave it to sit for an hour if you can. Cook whatever pasta you have on hand, drain and toss the pasta through the sauce.

Tomato tarts are what I make in summer when I really cannot be bothered cooking. I just take a sheet of puff pastry and cut it into rectangles, smear a bit of pesto on the pastry and pile chopped tomato on top (with small or cherry tomatoes, I don't even chop them, just cut them in half and place them cut-side up on top). Add salt and pepper, brush a bit of milk on the pastry if you can be bothered, and bake at 180°C until the pastry is golden, they take about 20 minutes. If I am feeling fancy, I smear Dijon mustard on the pastry, then chopped tomato, and top with grated Gruyère cheese.

Russian roulette
tomato salsa.

Oven-dried tomatoes: two ways

To make fast oven-dried tomatoes, I just cut tomatoes in half and arrange cut-side up on an oven tray. Add a splash of olive oil, a decent amount of salt and pepper and some sprigs of thyme if you have any. Cook in a 200°C oven until the tomatoes collapse and start to brown on top – cherry tomatoes take about 20 minutes, but big tomatoes need longer. I make them and use them quickly, either straight away or in the next day or two. You can stir them through pasta with torn basil and crumbled feta, smoosh them on toast or add them to an antipasto spread. You can also store them in the freezer and use them over the year like passata.

If you want to make oven-dried tomatoes more like the bought ones – chewy and intensely flavoured – you start in the same way. Halve tomatoes, cut-side up, splash of oil, salt and pepper. But you need to dry the fruit in a 100°C oven until they are properly dry and leathery. It can take several hours but, again, it very much depends on the size of the tomato, so keep an eye on them. Sometimes after a couple of hours of cooking, I press down on them with a fork to get the liquid out. When they are dry enough – you want them to be flexible but dry on the outside, if they still seem juicy put them back in the oven – pack them into glass jars and top off with olive oil. Add garlic cloves and sprigs of thyme, rosemary or oregano if you have them on hand.

Vegan basil pesto

My talented friend Sally Tagg, who has photographed gardens for *NZ Gardener* for many years and indeed took many of the photos that are used in this book, including the ones from my garden, gave me this recipe, which she was given by a vegan neighbour. Or rather the neighbour gave her some pesto and it was so delicious that Sally asked how it was made and has made it that way herself ever since. She has a collection of upcycled pots right by the back door of her home in Devonport, Auckland where she grows herbs specifically to make this and eats it all the time in summer.

Start with about 2 cups of green herbs. Sally uses mainly basil with some flat-leaf Italian parsley and rocket thrown in, but you can add chives, coriander, mint, chervil or tarragon if you have them and like them. Take ½ cup of whatever nuts or seeds you have (Sally usually uses walnuts or cashews) and dry-roast them in a frying pan (you can skip the dry-roasting, but Sally says the flavour of the pesto isn't as good).

Chop 2 cloves of garlic and blitz herbs with nuts or seeds, the chopped garlic and about ½ cup olive oil.

To make a non-vegan version, you can just add about ¼ cup of cheese. Sally often adds a teaspoon of vegan miso paste instead, which gives it that same full-flavoured umami taste that the cheese adds while keeping it vegan.

That second method of making oven-dried tomatoes keeps in the fridge for ages if the toms are dry enough. If they aren't, the fruit will start to decompose and fizz, so be warned.

Beans

Beans are a true workhorse of the summer garden. The plants produce pods in incredible abundance, especially climbing beans but even dwarf beans go like the clappers while they are producing.

They are easy from seed, easy to grow and all but pest-free too, although they are a little prone to sap-sucker infestations when they get too hot or dry out: consistent irrigation and mulch are the key to avoiding them.

I direct-sow climbing beans in mid spring and again at the start of the year to have strong young plants coming on and producing over late summer/early autumn when the older plants are slowing down. Like peas, the seed can be eaten by rats, mice or birds. If that happens you can start them in trays but they are so quick and easy to sow direct I would just protect the newly planted seed with something like plastic bottle cloches or a row cover while it gets going.

I sow dwarf beans (which are determinate so produce all their beans over a short period) successively, sowing a few every two or three weeks between mid-spring and midsummer so I always have more coming on. Dwarf beans don't need much in the way of staking (I mean they appreciate support if you give it to them, as we all do, but you can get away without it) so you can pop them into the garden wherever you have gaps; they are fine in pots too (see page 250).

Climbing beans, however, need about 2m of vertical support, so plant them at the base of something like a wigwam or a trellis. Lots of beans have a climbing and a dwarf form so you can pick 'n' mix what works for the space you have available.

Most beans are annual, so you need to plant each year, but 'Scarlet Runner' beans are perennial, which means they pop up every spring (although replace them after three or four years as the plants start to slow down). Pick 'Scarlet Runner' while the pods are young and tender, because they develop the characteristic fibrous strings – which need to be removed, bean by bean – if they get old and stringy. Or try 'Stringless Scarlet', bred from 'Scarlet Runner' and also perennial but pods stay tender and string-free.

I grow the climbing beans 'Shiny Fardenlosa' and 'Blue Lake Runner' and the dwarf bean 'Top Crop'. I also like the dwarf bean 'Coco White', which produces white navy or haricot beans. You can also grow shell out beans, where you eat the beans rather than the pods like broad beans, I like 'Climbing King George'; and beans that can be dried and stored for winter, such as 'Good Mother Stallard'. But actually some beans can be eaten as green beans (or rather snap beans, since they are not all green), shell out beans or dried and used as dried beans, it just depends at what stage they are picked.

Heritage Food Crops Research Trust in Whanganui has been tracking down rare heirloom beans from across New Zealand for years. Research director Mark Christensen told me they are preserving more than 80 rare bean varieties now, and some are available to home gardeners.

Bean harvests
at home. The dahlia is
'Penhill Watermelon'

Pick everything off continuously cropping edibles, like cherry tomatoes, before you go away.

Going on holiday

It would hardly be fair to suggest that gardeners never take a holiday in summer, but it must also be admitted that it's the very worst time to go away. Just a week or two of inattention can undo all the hard work you did over spring. If you must take a holiday – sometimes one's family insists, I know, I know – then water deeply and mulch well before you leave. It is an absolute arse to do but weed before you go too if you can: any weeds are competing with your desired edible crops for the limited available water. If you have crops in pots move them into a shady spot and rig up some shade cloth over crops growing in in-ground beds to slow the rate at which they transpire or use water.

Also pick as much as you can off continuously cropping fast growing edible like cucumbers, beans and zucchinis. I even pick cherry tomatoes, although bigger tomatoes take longer to ripen so I usually leave them on the vine. But if you leave the faster-growing vegetables on the plant to mature completely, the plant's production will slow right down – plants are only producing their edible pods or fruit because that's how they set seed for the next generation. If you leave the fruit to get completely ripe then the plant thinks its work is done and it goes into holiday mode too.

You can ask neighbours or friends to come and water the garden too, obviously! But even if you do that, take any steps you can to ensure your plants are not put under any additional stress from your absence. No one really waters your garden as well as you do, I find.

Cucumbers

Cucumbers are dangerously productive, you can harvest dozens of fruit off a single well-maintained plant. I start them from seed inside in mid spring, about September, and shift them out into the garden when it is reliably warm (between Labour weekend and mid-January in my Auckland garden, I wouldn't plant cucumber seedlings much later than early January in cooler places).

You can plant them as close as 30cm or 40cm apart if you train them to grow vertically. Or let them sprawl about the place but they take up room that way, leave about a metre between plants. Access to water is key for cukes, so water deeply at least twice a week and mulch around the plants. And pick the cucumbers while they are young, even if they are smaller than the ones you see in shops, they are far sweeter and crisper that way than if you let them get bloated and over-mature .

Cucumbers will eventually get powdery mildew. You can fuss about with baking soda and milk sprays but frankly I don't. It is inevitable in late summer, there is no point fighting it. But it's worth planting more seedlings in the second half of December, they should be producing when your earlier planted seedlings are running out of puff.

I grow 'Lebanese' green cucumber and the white round apple cucumber, as well as numerous pickling cucumbers to make homemade gherkins (see page 163). But there are lots of interesting cucumbers and they are all delightfully easy and productive.

You do see grafted cucumber seedlings but I am not sure if the extra expense is worth it for this crop, they are highly productive on their own roots. But if cucumbers are your favourite thing to eat and you get through a lot of them, splash out.

This is Nicky Fullick's tunnelhouse in Levin where she grows cucumbers vertically up a trellis. The marigolds are the Starfire Mix from Kings Seeds.

I make so many jars of gherkins a year that my partner Conrad once suggested I tender for the nationwide McDonald's franchise. He was joking, I think.

Gherkins

These are my absolute signature dish. Ideally grow actual pickling cucumbers, such as 'Homemade Pickles', 'Pick a Bushel', 'Eureka' or the imaginatively named 'Pickling Cucumber' if you want to make gherkins. They are just a shorter, wartier and less watery kind of cucumber and you can eat them fresh in salads just like regular cucumbers and if you leave them on the plant they get bigger. But if you are pickling them pick the fruit when it's about 6-8cm, any bigger and they get tricky to fit in regular-sized jars.

If you haven't grown pickling cucumbers, you can make this recipe out of ordinary cucumbers but because they are too big to fit in the jars you need to slice them up and I find they don't stay as crunchy.

Put your pickling cucumbers in a pot and cover with boiling water. Let it cool down. Then do it again at least once, possibly twice. Make a brine of one part sugar to two parts white vinegar – just scale this up depending on how many pickling cucumbers you have on hand – and add 1 tablespoon of salt for every cup of sugar you have used. Heat the brine until the sugar and salt has fully dissolved, then boil it for a minute or two.

Make up your own pickling spice with 4 tablespoons mustard seeds, 2 tablespoons allspice berries, 1 tablespoon coriander seeds, 12 cloves, 2 teaspoons ground ginger, 4 dried bay leaves, crumbled up (or the same number of fresh leaves used whole) and 4 cinnamon quills, broken up. That makes quite a lot of pickling spice so I can use it for several batches. You can use a bought pickling spice instead for this but honestly, the homemade pickling spice is the game-changer.

Drain the pickling cucumbers and pack them into hot sterilised jars. Try to get as many in a jar as you can, it looks better if they are packed in rather than floating about. Spoon a decent-sized spoonful of the pickling spice on top and then pour on the brine until the jars are absolutely full and all the gherkins are submerged. Wipe the tops of the jars to get rid of any stray seeds, then seal with sterilised lids. If the jars don't seal (you want to the lids to concave in on the top), I just store that jar in the fridge and use it up over the next month or so.

If you want homegrown gherkins, then grow, at an absolute minimum, six pickling cucumber plants – you can make gherkins a jar at a time, but six plants means you will be able to harvest enough gherks of the right size to fill a whole jar at once every couple of days.

Capsicums & Chillies

If you want to grow capsicums or chillies from seed, follow the exact same method as with tomatoes: they need it warm, warm, warm so start them inside, give them bottom heat while they are germinating if you can, or start them in a mini plastic bag greenhouse, then grow them on inside and don't shift them into the garden until the weather is settled and spring-like and the nights are reliably warm. Don't be in a rush to get them outside.

Having said that, I find both take a long time to fruit, you are usually waiting for three months or so after planting for standard chillies and smaller-fruited capsicums, longer for the bigger ones. In regions with short summers, I'd keep them in pots (see page 250). Not only will the soil in pots be warmer, you can shift pots to take advantage of the microclimates your garden offers. Somewhere like the base of a north-facing wall, especially if the wall is brick, stone or concrete and so has a bit of thermal mass, will get sun all day, plus the wall will trap heat from the sun and release it overnight. That's not a bad situation for them even in warmer regions to be honest, the best crop I ever had was grown at the base of a north facing wall of my brick house in Auckland. These plants like to stay warm. Plus growing them in pots means you can try and overwinter them to grow on the following year (see page 250).

I don't normally stake chillies, which produce small fruit, but stake capsicums when you plant them, especially if you are growing the ones with big supermarket capsicum-like fruit, such as 'California Wonder', 'Jumbo' or 'Giant Bell'. The branches are pretty fragile, I find, and can bend and snap with the weight of the fruit or in the wind. I usually don't bother growing the bigger capsicums though, I find the smaller fruited varieties are more productive and can be used in just the same way when you are cooking (unless you want to make stuffed peppers, in which case I hope the 1970s are going well for you). I like 'Jingle Bells' and this year I tried 'Dwarf Snack Orange', which is sweet enough to eat raw like an apple. Last year I also grew 'Cornos', a red sweet pepper shaped like a carrot, which I smoked over charcoal

Some years I grow 'Alma', a paprika pepper that you can dry and grind to make homemade paprika. I started growing it after Setha Davenport from Setha's Seeds in Hawke's Bay told me she grew it, and that homegrown paprika was so nice she could hardly resist eating it straight from the jar. I agree, it's delicious, The fruit on this does take ages to ripen though, a good four months for me.

The pepper I am picking is 'Dwarf Snack Orange'. They are very sweet and you can eat the fruit raw, so they are great for kids' lunchboxes.

Harvesting chillies. Last year I grew one that was so hot, I could only pick it with garden gloves on!

to make homegrown roasted red peppers like you buy in jars. Just put the whole fruit on the grill over charcoal at the ember stage, and once the peppers are blackened, pop them into a bowl to cool. After that you can peel off the blackened skin and remove the seeds easily. They keep in the fridge for a week or so, but you can also freeze them in sealable bags.

I love chillies. Every year I plant at least eight plants which is simply bananas as two chilli plants would easily supply even a heavy chilli user like me for the whole year: you can just throw chillies in the freezer and take them out and use them over the year.

If you are only going to grow one, I'd just buy a 'Wildfire' seedling, it's massively productive. But why only grow one, my friend? 'Bird's Eye' is good, producing tiny but hot chillies; 'Sky Hot' chillies are so bright red they look like they are painted; 'Jalapeño' chillies range between mild and hot and can be smoked to make your own chipotle. I love the super-hot chillies, such as 'Bhut Jolokia', 'Carolina Reaper' and 'Scotch Bonnet', just be aware they are both slower and more tropical than the milder chillies.

I find they need about a month longer for the fruit to ripen and they really cannot take the cold, down south I would keep them in undercover even if you grow regular chillies outside (If you live in a cooler region with a shorter summer, try the perennial and cold-tolerant 'Rocoto').

Keep picking chillies to keep the plant setting fruit. But if you want hot chillies, leave the fruit on the plant as long as you can. The level of capsaicin, which is what makes chillies hot, continues to increase.

Zucchini

Zucchini grow before your eyes. Most years, the challenge isn't so much growing them it is using them up, and/or palming them off on unsuspecting neighbours. Treat this crop very like their cucurbit cousin, the cucumber: if you are starting them from seed, do it inside in around mid-spring and shift them into the garden when it is reliably warm. They will only start setting fruit when it is warm enough, there's really no point trying to get a jump on the season. In terms of production, one plant per person is usually enough, although I find you get better fruit set if you grow two near each other. Anyway if you are only growing one or two, I'd say go for a basic green F1 hybrid like 'Black Jack' or 'Black Beauty'. There are all sorts of fun zucchini, but none are as productive as those basic green ones, I find. But if you have the space to grow a few: there are striped ones ('Cocozelle'), pure gold ones ('Gold Rush'), spaceship-shaped ones (any scallopini), bicoloured ones ('Zephyr' is golden yellow but looks like it has had its bottom half dipped in pale green paint) and even a climbing one ('Rampicante', also known as the 'Tromboncino' squash, which matures into trombone-shaped butternut fruit). Zucchini tend to sprawl all over the place, so I try to train them vertically as otherwise they take up all the space in my intensively planted garden. Stake when you plant them and as the plant grows, tie the stem up the stake. Remove all of the leaves that form below the lowest fruit. You end up with a long stem with foliage and fruit in a ring at the top, like a palm tree.

'Rampicante' grows like a weed, its prolific nature deserves to be remarked on even among zucchinis. Eat the young fruit like any old zucchini or leave the fruit to mature on the vine until the skin hardens then you can store it like a winter squash (to which it is closely related).

Zucchini flowers are edible, but pick the male flowers to eat (leaving a few for pollination) or you'll have fewer fruit. Female flowers have a bulb at the bottom of the flower.

Sweetcorn is ready to pick when the tassels at the end turn brown.

Sweetcorn

Homegrown sweetcorn will, truly, blow your mind. The sugar in the cobs starts to convert to starch after it is picked. So quickly does that change the taste of corn, that I read something years ago that you should have the water boiling before you even go outside to pick it and I always try to do that.

I am not actually sure if the timing is quite that critical but it's true that fresh picked corn is noticeably sweeter.

Corn likes it warm. Sometimes I start it in trays in mid spring, sometimes I sow it direct in late spring (although it's one of those nutrient-dense seeds that everything seems to dig up and eat so protect newly sown seeds as with peas or beans).

Whether you are sowing or planting, this is a crop you need to grow in blocks, with plants about 30cm apart, rather than rows: it is wind-pollinated and each individual kernel need to be pollinated. If you harvest corn with gappy kernels, it's a pollination issue.

I often find it hard to achieve perfect pollination when growing corn on a small scale at home: I imagine with a whole field of corn there is pollen everywhere, in my little urban garden there is just not enough floating about.

But you can help things along after the tassels, or male flowers, at the top of the plant have formed by gently shaking or tapping the stalks each time you pass by.

It mimics the action of the wind and helps the pollen in the male flowers to be released.

Even in my small household, I find it quite hard to grow enough to supply our own needs. I usually get between one and two cobs on each stalk, sometimes three, but I find on the modern corn varieties there is usually only one good cob, any others are smaller. But you can and should grow corn successively if you have the space to do so. Sow or plant another block every two or three weeks. I stop planting corn in early January in my Auckland garden, in regions with shorter summers you might want to stop by mid-December.

There are lots of modern hybrids that produce classic yellow cobs, try 'Chieftan', 'Honey and Pearl' or the sweet 'NZ Yellow'. But there are also heirloom corn varieties to dry and grind for flour (like 'Glass Gem', 'Painted Mountain' or 'Blue Hopi'). Actually, 'Glass Gem' and 'Painted Mountain' both produce cobs with multicoloured kernels, they are so pretty you might want to dry them and keep them as ornaments.

You can also grow popcorn. You can't just dry any corn, it has to be a flint corn. But look out for the corns 'Popcorn Ruby Red', 'Popcorn Mushroom' or 'Pop Star' ('Glass Gem' makes good popcorn too). Let cobs dry fully on the plant, it makes it easier to twist the kernels off.

Autumn scenes. The terracotta rhubarb forcer was a gift from Dot Smith who owns Riverstone Castle in Oamaru.

Autumn harvests

The days are getting shorter and the nights cooler but early autumn is when my garden is in peak production, so there is masses to pick and preserve.

Spring gets the glory but eating from the garden year-round comes down to what you do in autumn.

t is tempting, I know, to garden in bursts. In early spring, when the sun is shining, you can feel the sap rising in you and it stirs you to get out and get your hands in the soil and plant and sow everything you can get your greenfingers on.

And look, that's one way to do it. If, for you, gardening is to blitz the garden over Labour weekend leaving you free to focus on other pursuits for the rest of the year, no judgement my friend. Indeed, I was talking to my friend Robert Guyton, who has a food forest in Riverton, and he was telling me about the tradition of paddock gardens, where a farmer fences off a paddock in spring, runs the tractor over it and then plants it all in one go on one day with every crop he or she wants to grow for the year. (He says it's tremendously productive but I don't have a spare paddock to try it myself),

In my garden I too am prone to spring fever – the worst symptom for me is impulsive plant-buying with no plan at all of where things will grow. And to an extent it works fine: you can still produce a lot of food. But if you plant a lot on one day you naturally tend have a lot that is ready all at once. You end up with a glut of one thing or another, desperately hustling to get it processed or preserved or give it away, so it isn't wasted.

Increasingly I have come to see that a steady production of edible crops from the garden requires more of a little-and-often-approach.

I was listening to a podcast where the British gardener Monty Don said the absolute secret to vegetable-gardening success was to have a plan for the whole year ahead and do something towards it every day.

That really stayed with me. It felt almost impossible when I first heard it. But it is easier than you might think. As you pick something, sow or plant something. Pull a few weeds as you walk past. It doesn't have to be a lot to make a radical difference.

As the weather gets colder and light levels drop in autumn, growth slows right down. It's hard to believe at the start of autumn, when the garden is hugely productive, but you know it's going to happen, and you need to plan for it and plant for it. To have veges over winter, and even early spring – the so-called 'hungry gap' when there's very little in the garden that is ready to eat – you need to have them in early enough that they are a decent size with a strong, established root system when growth slows down. Nothing will grow much more over winter, but that means they will shoot away as soon as it warms up in spring.

Robert Guyton
in his Riverton
food forest.

Clockwise from top left: Sowing seed; thin seedlings planted too closely; harvesting; the edible leaves.

Beetroot

For quite a few years I never grew beetroot. I had the idea I didn't like it because I had been scarred by the canned, vinegary sort you used to get in takeaway burgers. But homegrown beetroot tastes quite different to that, it has the same sweetness as carrots to me just a bit earthier. I start sowing it direct as soon as the soil temperature allows, which might be late winter or early spring for me in Auckland but wait for spring proper down south. My favourite variety is 'Chioggia', which has red and white rings like a concentric candy cane, but I also like 'Bulls Blood', which has dark red leaves, and 'Cylindra' is great if you want to bottle it (it's shaped like a torpedo rather than a globe, so it fits nicely into jars). Even if you space them perfectly, be aware that beetroot seed is naturally multigerm: each seed is actually a little cluster of two to four embryos so you need to thin after they germinate so they have room to swell up underground. You can eat any you pull out as microgreens – the whole plant is edible – but they ones you are growing for the roots need the leaves to photosynthesise, so don't pinch too many of them for your salads.

If you don't like thinning seedlings, look out for the beetroot varieties 'Kestrel' or 'Moulin Rouge', both of which have monogerm seeds that contain only one embryo. You can also splash out on seed tape, which is always perfectly spaced.

Eggplants

I love eggplants even though they are almighty divas in the garden and only hit and miss for me on their own roots. They really do like it warm – I was talking to a commercial eggplant grower a few years ago who told me the glasshouse he grew them in was kept at 19°C at night and up to 27°C during the day and in the garden, they simply won't set fruit unless the day-time temperature is averaging above 23°C.

If I am starting them from seed, I follow basically the same process as tomatoes but in every way eggplants demand more of you. I start them earlier, usually in August, and the seed needs even more warmth to strike: use a seedling heat mat if you have one.

If you are growing in trays, you will need to pot the seedlings on into individual pots to grow on inside or undercover for several more weeks – I usually direct sow into pots so I can skip the potting on step. If you do that, sow two or three seeds in each pot and then select the strongest growing one in each pot soon after germination. They need a long hot season to produce fruit so it's a bit of balance as to when to plant them outside really: you want to make sure you get them planted before the soil starts to dry off in summer and so you can get a crop before it starts to get cool again, but also wait until it's warm enough for them. In colder places you will have to keep them undercover or in pots so you can shift them into your hothouse at the start and end of the season. I grow them outside in my Auckland garden, but as with tomatoes, I wait until it's warm enough to sit outside in the evening without needing a hoodie to plant them out. On top of that I often grow them in 40L black plastic pots to raise the soil temperature for them a little.

If you want to grow them in beds, or in the ground, you could also use a mulch of black plastic over the soil to keep it warm for them. When you do plant them outside though, bury them deeply, like tomatoes, so the stem is buried up to the first leaves so they can develop a bigger, stronger root system: unless you are growing a grafted eggplant (see page 182), in which case make sure you don't bury the graft.

If you don't have a seedling heat mat, you can use plastic wrap to make a mini hothouse for your seed trays or my friend Jack Hobbs from Auckland Botanic Gardens told me he piles grass clippings into a tub (something like a Gubba flexi tub) then adds a layer of sand and sites his seed trays for eggplants on top of that and keeps the whole thing in his hothouse. The grass breaks down, which generates heat, which radiates up through the sand.

Harvest eggplants
with secateurs, rather
than pulling the fruit
off the plants.

Clockwise from top left: Seedlings; the flowers; eggplants will grow in pots; stake well.

Stake them at the time of planting, especially if you are growing the sort with bigger fruit.

In the garden, I feed them like tomatoes, literally with the same dilute liquid tomato fertiliser every couple of weeks (tomato fertiliser is high in potassium, which will support the development of buds, flowers and fruit in anything, not just tomatoes, I basically use the same fertiliser on all fruiting plants, including peppers, chillies, pumpkins, cucumbers, zucchinis and beans). I usually give them a side dressing of compost a couple of times over the growing season too.

Once they start flowering, you sometimes need to help pollination along: the pollen in the flowers of eggplants is held inside tubes and only able to be released when the flower is vibrated at a particular frequency, they have evolved to attract what are called buzz pollinators such a bumblebees. So, you can dab a paintbrush around in one flower then another, or replicate buzz pollination with an electric toothbrush – just remove the brush head and touch the metal part to the open centre of each flower, allowing it to vibrate against the bloom for a few seconds. Blueberries, tomatoes, chillies and peppers are all buzz-pollinated, so try the same trick with them too.

Once you get over their neurotic neediness and demanding personalities, there is actually a lot to recommend eggplants as garden plants. For a start they are simply stunning. Indeed, the first reference to them in seed catalogues in the UK listed them among ornamental plants. I love the glossy purple supermarket-style varieties where the fruit is as shiny as oil like 'Black King', 'Early Prolific' or 'Black Beauty', but there's all sorts of colours and shapes. There are green ones like 'Thai Green Egg' or 'Rabi Long Green'; white varieties like 'White Star'; and stripy ones like 'Tsakoniki'.

In general, the smaller varieties are faster to fruit and more prolific and all round a better choice in marginal climates. Even when I grow the bigger varieties outside at home the fruit never gets as big as the eggplants you see in supermarkets grown in those tropical hothouses, so don't worry if the fruit seems small.

Knowing when to harvest takes a bit of practice, the fruit should be firm and shiny and give a little if you press the fruit with your thumb but bounce back. If you let them become overripe, they will start to lose their sheen and feel spongy.

If you want to grow an eggplant in a container, there's a prolific hybrid variety 'Patio Baby' bred to grow well in pots; one year I harvested at least two dozen fruit off the one plant.

Give grafted a go, guys

Grafting is a kind of propagation where the top part of one plant (scion) is joined onto the bottom part of another (rootstock), and the two parts grow into one plant that has desirable qualities from the rootstock – such as extra vigour, greater yield and/or better disease-resistance – while still maintaining the desired qualities of the scion – such as the fruit, flowers and leaves. So, you might get the old-fashioned flavour of an heirloom tomato on a plant that grows as fast and as vigorously as an F1 hybrid.

Various plants are grafted – fruit trees often are, as are roses – but tomatoes, eggplants, cucumbers and capsicums are all available as grafted seedlings, and you also see grafted rockmelons and watermelons.

"It's like putting a Formula One race car on a Land Rover chassis," Paul Wylaars from Zealandia Horticulture told me. "You've got the best of both worlds. Great taste, great flavour on top. But when the road suddenly gets rough and the plant is facing a bit of disease pressure or it's too wet, the plant can get through it. Whereas an ungrafted plant, facing those same conditions, would probably weaken and get a disease or possibly die."

Now grafted seedlings are more expensive, as obviously splicing two plants together is way more complicated than simply growing something from seed. In terms of the yield, I think you get value for money too. I have grown the bigger varieties of eggplants from seed, but I wouldn't bother again unless I was able to grow them undercover for the whole season. Growing them outside, I got about a quarter as much fruit as a grafted plant that same year.

And grafted plants often grow with such vigour they avoid altogether some problems that same plant on its own roots is prone to, in particular soil-borne diseases, which they often totally swerve. Grafted tomatoes have such a strong and vigorous root system you can even be lazier about taking laterals off. You still have to do it sometimes or they grow into a complete forest, but you can run two or three laterals off the one plant rather than stake it to a single vine.

I grow lots of grafted veges, particularly grafted eggplants since they are such divas, but I usually put in a few grafted tomatoes, which start fruiting before my seed-raised ones do and maybe a grafted pepper for the same reason. If you are new to gardening; have a small garden and need everything to produce to its maximum potential; are growing in pots, which is basically a more stressful environment for plants; or are growing something in a climate that is marginal for it, I fully recommend grafted plants. In fact, I just recommend them generally.

With grafted plants, don't bury the graft, where the scion meets the rootstock. You can see it – it's like a knot in the stem. If buried, the rootstock can start sending up top growth and since the rootstock is chosen for bumptious vigour, that is likely to overwhelm the variety you want.

A **very** productive grafted eggplant.

Outstanding
eggplant brinjal.

Eggplant brinjal

This recipe was passed on to me by the Waikato food writer Rowan Bishop. I had fallen in love with a feijoa chutney recipe of hers – I have a huge feijoa tree, and I am always on the hunt for recipes that do not require you to peel the feijoas (that huge feijoa tree has produced thousands of fruit every year for years so the thought of peeling another feijoa frankly fails to thrill). Anyway, I got in touch with Rowan to tell her how much I liked that feijoa chutney (see page 186), and she said I had to try making her eggplant brinjal recipe and passed it along. So I did and it is just sensational, now I make it every year. In fact I struggle to make enough as we just burn through it.

2 large eggplants, about 500g each
4 teaspoons salt
1 cup oil
¼ cup yellow mustard seeds
2 tablespoons fenugreek seeds
2 tablespoons coriander seeds
2 tablespoons cumin seeds
100g crushed garlic
100g minced ginger
1 tablespoon chilli powder
3 x 410g tins peeled tomatoes
  in juice, chopped
¼ cup tamarind paste
1 cup malt vinegar
1kg sugar

Slice the unpeeled eggplant into small (5mm) dice. Place in a colander, sprinkled evenly with the salt. Set aside over a sink or bowl to drain for 30 minutes.

Heat the oil in a large, heavy-based pot or jam pan over a medium-high heat. Add the mustard seeds and heat until they start to pop. Remove from the heat and stir in the fenugreek, coriander and cumin seeds followed by the garlic, ginger and chilli powder. Return to a lowered heat and cook, stirring, for about 4 minutes. Stir in the salted and drained eggplant without rinsing or patting dry - just shake the colander before adding the eggplant, then sauté for 3-4 minutes.

Stir in the chopped tomatoes with juice, tamarind paste, vinegar and the sugar.

Simmer the mixture, uncovered, for about 1½ hours, stirring occasionally. Oil should rise to the surface after about an hour, and further cooking produces a medium-thick chutney, reduced to almost half the original volume.

Bottle in hot, sterilised jars with hot, sterilised screw-on lids.

You can buy tamarind paste from Asian outlets or sometimes in the international aisle at the supermarket; Rowan recommends the Pantainorasingh brand.

Feijoa, lime and smoked paprika chutney

I know, I know, we are talking about growing vegetables rather than fruit but I thought I had better include the feijoa recipe from Rowan I mentioned too, it's a huge favourite of mine. If you have a feijoa tree, you always need more recipes that don't involve peeling anything. With the time you save you can learn a language or something.

700g peeled onions, chopped
8 red chillies
2 limes
1 large red capsicum, chopped
200ml red wine vinegar
300ml orange juice
3kg feijoas
20 makrut lime leaves
1kg white sugar
500g brown sugar
1 cinnamon quill, roughly broken
1 tablespoon whole coriander seeds
1¼ teaspoons chilli powder
2 teaspoons dulce (or sweet)
  smoked paprika

Place onions, chillies and limes in a food processor and process until chopped but not puréed. Add to a pot with capsicum, red wine vinegar and orange juice. Stir to mix and set over a low heat. Top and tail unpeeled feijoas, dice them into 1cm cubes and add to the pot along with makrut lime leaves, white sugar, brown sugar, cinnamon quill, coriander seeds, chilli powder and paprika. Bring to the boil, simmer for 2 hours, pour into jars and seal.

Ugly carrot and lentil soup

Sometimes I leave carrots in the ground over winter. I just throw a layer of pea straw mulch over the top of them in autumn and they store fine in the soil in my Auckland garden, so long as you lift them before spring as these biennials will try to flower if you let them grow on for a second season and then the edible root will taste bitter. If you live somewhere where the soil freezes in winter I'd lift them before that happens, as they'll turn to mush if they freeze and then thaw. Anyway, if I leave them in the soil too long and they get a bit hairy and ugly looking, I use them to make this soup. You blitz it at the end and it tastes delicious, whether or not your carrots meet any socially constructed vegetable beauty standards.

I throw about 500g of carrots with the dirt washed off into my slow cooker. It can be more or less, depending on how many carrots you have, this is a very flexible recipe. You don't need to peel the carrots, or at any rate, I never do, but if they are big chunky ones I chop them into two or three pieces. I add 1 tablespoon of cumin seeds, about a cup of red lentils, a splash of olive oil or a spoon of butter, salt and pepper and about a litre or so of stock. Sometimes I throw a teaspoon or so of chilli flakes in too. Cook on high for two or three hours until the carrots and lentils are completely soft, then blitz with the stick blender to make a smooth soup. If I make a big batch of this and store it in the fridge for a couple of days, the lentils make it thicken up, which I like – it feels very hearty and filling. Stir some yoghurt through just before you serve it.

Feijoa, lime and smoked paprika chutney.

This is the little round carrot 'Paris Market'.

Carrots

Carrots are a real boogieman crop for some people. I know Yotam Kay from Pakaraka Permaculture in Thames told me carrots were one of the most common things he was asked about when he and Niva ran home gardening workshops. The secret, he says, is to ensure the ground is kept continuously moist for the two weeks or so while they are germinating: he suggests you sow just before rain is forecast and growing in spring and autumn when there is naturally more moisture in the soil. You could theoretically sow carrots year-round in mild regions, and from spring until late summer in colder ones. But I usually only sow them in Auckland from late spring until early autumn, I find the germination is slow and patchy when the soil is cold and they grow so slowly over winter I'd rather use the space for something else. I like 'Scarlet Nantes' and 'Tendersweet', and I often grow the little round carrot, 'Paris Market', since you don't have to worry about it forking.

Carrot seed is absolutely tiny and I find it impossible to space by eye. So, because I hate faffing about thinning plants that I have sown too close together, I make a trench about 10cm deep and backfill with sand and potting mix, then I mark holes with the tines of a rake and use a bought seed dispenser to space the tiny seed perfectly (you can buy a seed dispenser at any garden centre, they are just a few dollars). If you don't have a seed dispenser, you can also buy carrot seed tape where the seed is already spaced, it's a little bit more expensive but given it takes a whole job off the future to-do list, I sometimes splash out.

You don't want to be thinning carrots a lot, even though they are difficult to space. Even time you thin, you will damage the foliage of the seedlings you pull up and the scent of that attracts carrot fly.

Slugs and snails just love carrots, so I use a bird-safe slug bait when I sow them. If you have a row cover made of horticultural mesh (see page 137) you can use that to protect the carrots from carrot fly.

Kate's carrot salad

This is a recipe from my sister Kate. She has been a vegetarian since she was 11 and is always on the hunt for interesting salads. She tried a carrot salad in a café, and it was so good she tried to replicate it at home. This is easy and incredibly good, Kate is always asked to bring it to potlucks. You can use any fresh herbs you happen to have. Kate says coriander is the classic, but she's made it with parsley, mint and a combo of all.

½ cup threaded coconut
1 cup raw almonds (or cashews)
2 teaspoons ground coriander
2 tablespoons oil
4-5 carrots, grated
Small bunch of fresh herbs, chopped

Dressing
Juice of 1 lemon
¼ cup olive oil
3 cloves garlic, crushed
1 teaspoon salt

Combine the coconut, nuts, ground coriander and first measure of oil in a bowl.

Put onto an oven tray and bake at 150°C for 10 minutes or until just brown. When it smells nice and toasty it is done. You can also do this in an air fryer for 6-8 minutes.

Grate carrots. Kate uses a julienne grater to make it fancy if she is taking it to a barbecue.

Throw the salad ingredients all together in a bowl. For the dressing, chuck all ingredients in a jar and shake it up. Add the dressing to the salad just before serving.

Mushrooms on toast like in a café

My mother Rosaleen loves having creamy mushrooms on toast in a café so she worked out this method of making it below, which comes out very creamy although it contains no cream or crème fraîche. Now if you ever order mushrooms on toast in a café with her, she gives a short TED talk about how the version she makes is actually much nicer.

1 tablespoon olive oil
1 clove garlic, chopped (Mum actually
  uses a sprinkle of powdered garlic)
About 400-500g mushrooms, chopped
A handful of flat-leaf parsley, chopped
A smaller handful of fresh thyme sprigs
  (you can chop it, or pull each sprig between
  your finger and thumb to get the leaves off)
Salt and pepper

Add oil and garlic to a cold pan. Put pan over a medium heat and cook the garlic, stirring constantly, until the garlic is pale gold (the cold pan is a good trick, it stops the garlic from burning, I do the same thing when sautéing onions too). Add the mushrooms, with a splash more olive oil if needed. Reduce the heat a little and cook for about 10 or so minutes, stirring often. Add chopped parsley and thyme leaves and salt and pepper to taste and cook for another 5 minutes or so. Serve on toast.

Bart says that shiitake are one of the easiest and most productive mushrooms to grow on logs at home.

Mushrooms

Bart Acres, who is the founder of MycoLogic in Dunedin, told me there are three ways to grow mushrooms at home. You can make mushroom grow logs – cut suitable logs of the right size, drill holes, and insert mushroom culture dowels then tuck the whole thing in a shady corner: they will start cropping after a year.

For mushrooms that do not like to grow in logs, you can also make an outdoor patch in your garden, by laying down a wheelbarrow load or two of the appropriate substrate and inoculating it with the spawn of the species you are trying to grow (you need about 1kg of spawn per 1sqm) and that should start cropping in 9-12 months.

And finally, you can grow them in grow kits, bags or buckets. You can set one up yourself with a food-grade bucket: just drill a few holes in the side and pack it full of oyster mushroom grain spawn and pasteurised straw (you pasteurise straw by soaking it in a solution of water and hydrated lime or in very hot water, between 70 and 80°C). That will produce mushrooms in about two weeks.

I have to confess, the only way I have grown mushrooms is with a pre-made mushroom grow kit but I recommend that highly: it's very easy, takes almost no space and you produce an abundance of absolutely delicious mushrooms.

You can buy grow kits for a whole range of mushrooms. Look out for options that will let you grow grey oyster mushrooms; shiitake; native phoenix oysters; pink oyster mushrooms; or the native pekepeke-kiore.

Kūmara

Kūmara grow from shoots, sometimes called runners or tipu. You can buy them but it's easy to produce them yourself. Just lie four or five kūmara not touching each other on a bed of mixed straw and soil in something like a banana box and then cover with soil. Keep the box moist but not wet and in a warm place and your tipu will be ready to plant in late spring or early summer. You should get about 10 or 15 tipu per kūmara so you'll have loads to plant and give away.

Just prise them gently off the mother tuber when they are about 10-15cm long and ideally pop them in a jar of water or seaweed tea so the bottom end is just submerged for a few days until the roots are growing strongly (you don't want the roots to dry out, they are quite delicate).

You can also just upend a single kūmara over a jar of water so the bottom end is submerged, and refresh the water every couple of days. Eventually the tipu will form.

Professor Nick Roskruge from Massey University, chair of Tāhuri Whenua, the National Māori Vegetable Growers Collective, told me the key to success with kūmara is in the timing: as in the soil needs to be warm enough for them but you can't leave it too long to get the tipu in the ground as they need a long and warm summer to produce – they take about five months from planting to harvest. So produce the tipu early enough that you have them ready to plant as soon as the conditions are warm enough.

If you can't guarantee five months of warm weather, I have heard from gardeners down south producing them undercover. They also do very well in big containers or grow bags in marginal climates, provided you keep the soil damp. The tubers are usually smaller but it makes harvesting easier as you can tip the whole lot out. In fact in some ways they suit growing in containers: kūmara likes perfect drainage and then to hit a hard surface in order to form roots. If you are growing in the ground, sandy soil over hardpan would be ideal. In fact, if you have lovely friable soil, or you dig over too well prior to planting, the roots can go down forever and harvesting the tubers involves significant excavation!

Traditionally kūmara was grown in puke or mounds, you can also make a raised long ridge. To plant the tipu, make a shallow well at the base of the mound or ridge and lie the tipu down flat then fill in the well so the top half is vertical like it is sitting upright. It's often referred to as planting in a J-shape.

If they are in the ground, kūmara will scramble all over the show, lift the vines regularly or they will put down roots wherever they touch the soil. Harvest before the first frost and when the weather is dry: the tubers need to cure in the sun in order to store well.

NZ Gardener's **deputy editor** Mei Leng Wong often sprouts a kūmara in her kitchen over winter and harvests the edible leaves: she throws them in soups, stir-fries them with chilli and garlic, or uses them raw in the Malaysian or Indonesian salad, ulam.

Lift the tubers carefully by hand. If they get nicked by metal tools they won't store as well.

Pumpkin vines are productive but they do sprawl.

Pumpkins

Pumpkins are very easy to grow, in fact they often grow themselves from the compost heap which is useful in a couple of ways. Firstly, it involves zero effort or time from you and secondly it usually means they are growing in an out-of-the-way spot in the garden, whereas in the vegetable beds they can scramble all over the shop and overwhelm everything else. If they don't oblige by simply appearing on or near your compost, you can also plant them there on purpose, provided it's in a sunny spot. If you live rurally try them at the base of a pile of old horse manure (or chicken or cow, just whatever poo you happen to have) or on the site of an old burn pile. There are smaller varieties for compact spaces, try 'Golden Nugget', which grows more like a bush than a vine. You can also train them vertically (see page 234) although again only plant the smaller fruiting sorts if you do, even a medium-sized pumpkin weighs enough to pull the vine off the support.

They are fun to sow from seed, as the seed is big and easy to handle, this is a great crop to start with kids. They take a while to produce fruit – the smaller-fruiting varieties are quicker but even they are not what I would call fast – but once they get going they are massively prolific: one year I planted exactly two (from seed) and gave them barely any attention and I harvested easily more than 40 kilos (good gourd, I heard you say) of pumpkins.

Start seed inside in spring and plant out towards the end of spring, beginning of summer. They like it warm, sometimes I don't plant them outside until November or December at which stage I either transplant seedlings or just sow direct. I'd even plant the smaller, quicker-fruiting varieties in January in my Auckland garden, although if you have a shorter summer that might be on the late side, try and get them in before Christmas.

If you want to grow them to store, it's hard to beat the classic grey blue iron bark sorts. 'Whangaparoa Crown' is a great keeper or 'Queensland Blue'. I love 'Musquee de Provence', which, to me, looks exactly like the pumpkin that Cinderella's carriage is made from (there are actually

There is an Australian heirloom vegetable seed company called the Diggers Club and I was in Australia talking to its founder Clive Blazey years ago about pumpkins. He described a particular kind of iron bark pumpkin as more thick-skinned than a politician and now I always describe them that way too.

a few French heirlooms varieties that look like that, they are often classed as cinderella pumpkins).

I like butternuts too, try 'Butterscotch' or 'Chieftain'. Although since I have a small household, I grow the adorable 'Butter Baby', which produces darling little fruit as long as your hand that the two of us can easily eat.

I also like the New Zealand heirloom squash kamo kamo or sometimes kumi kumi. Hanui Lawrence, who established and maintains Aunty's Garden at Waipatu Marae in Hastings (for a koha, locals can pick their own spray-free produce) told me the secret to delicious kamo kamo was harvesting it when it's small – not much bigger than an apple – for the best flavour, and steaming it.

Whatever you are growing, once the fruit appears, put a piece of cardboard or board or something under it, if it is sitting directly on the soil it is liable to rot. Turn the fruit regularly, in so far as possible, so as much of the skin as possible is exposed to the sun.

It is tempting to pick pumpkins much earlier than you should. In late summer they get powdery mildew (like all cucurbits) and start to look just awful.

But sit on your hands and leave them on the vine as long as you can. Don't cut the leaves that are affected by powdery mildew off the vine either, they are still feeding the pumpkins. When the leaves would basically crumble to dust when you touch them you can harvest the pumpkins, or when the stems of the fruit are almost completely dried off and is brown. When you do harvest them, leave a decent length of the vine attached to the stem, especially if you are growing them to store – if you cut the vine too short it can allow rot to set in.

Leave pumpkins on the vine as long as you can, and even after you harvest, leave the fruit to cure for another two or three weeks. It massively improves the flavour, and means they store better and for longer too, so your patience will be well rewarded.

Clockwise from top left: Prop the fruit up on something like cardboard; Candy Harris' amazing pumpkin harvest in Clarkville; gourds growing vertically; Randolf and Marty Holst's pumpkin vine in Wānaka.

Clockwise from top left: Yam harvests; Roddy Branagan, co-founder of Setha's Seeds in Hawke's Bay, harvesting yams; Jerusalem artichoke harvest; the daisy-like yellow flowers.

Yams

Yams are so easy and productive it's almost a problem: part of the oxalis family, they can spread a little too vigorously! But if you have an unused weedy corner, use them as a weed control. Wellington gardener Elien Lewis told me she had a spot in her garden that was difficult to access and hard to keep tidy, so one spring she cleared as much as she could, threw down some supermarket-bought yams and covered them with chopped plant mulch and compost. In winter when the foliage died away she harvested a bumper crop. She did mention every yam left behind goes on to sprout the following year (and you will leave a few behind, no matter how carefully you look), so it's not the best option for space you want to grow other things in but a great choice for any unused space.

Jerusalem artichokes

Treat Jerusalem artichokes exactly like yams. Plant them in spring (even late winter in warmer regions) and they will be ready to harvest in late autumn but you can leave them in the ground over winter and just dig them up as you need them. If you leave any tubers in the ground (and again: you absolutely will) they will come up the next year, so once again find an out-of-the-way, underused spot for them. They are not actually related to artichokes (or indeed from Jerusalem), they are part of the sunflower family: they send up tall (2 or 3m) daisy-like yellow flowers in summer so make sure they won't shade anything else you are growing. This is a very easy crop with only one downside really: Jerusalem artichokes contain high levels of inulin, which is a non-digestible carbohydrate that causes gas. People often call them fartichokes. I will say no more.

Silverbeet is biennial, although it's usually grown as an annual in New Zealand. I leave a couple of plants to grow for the second year so it can self-seed, which it does freely from towering, twisting seedheads.

Winter is coming

You can plant and sow veges over winter, but everything in the garden is slowing down and there is probably a lesson in that for us all.

Gardening in winter teaches you both patience and the benefit of forward planning.

t's entirely possible to eat from your garden all winter. But if you have left it until winter to do anything about it you probably won't be eating much, to be honest.

This is the season that separates the deliberate planners from the spur-of-the-moment planters. Because having veges ready to go over the colder months requires thinking ahead, and planning and planting so you have anticipated what you'll need for your winter soups while on summer hols.

That's not to say you can't still plant and sow some edible crops over the winter months – you can. So long as the soil isn't frozen, tough legumes like broad beans and peas will still grow, you can plant New Zealand spinach and silverbeet seedlings as well as some edible alliums, some brassicas, and various leafy things like mizuna, tatsoi, corn salad and pak choi. I have lettuces in pots on the go over winter too. I keep picking from them and they keep producing but to be fair their progress is slow.

But then everything grows much more slowly in winter than it does over the rest of the year. Not just because it's colder, although that is part of it. But also the light levels are lower, and the shadows are longer. Soil microbes slow down too so it takes longer for organic matter to break down into a form that plants can take up.

I don't mind things slowing down over winter. There's a rightness to it, a certain relief even. The rest of the year can be a blur of rushing to get seed sown and seedlings planted, then you're under the pump getting all the edible crops harvested and eaten or preserved to eat while pickings are leaner.

Frankly, by winter, I want to slow down too. With less to distract you happening in the short-term in the garden, you can think long-term, plant trees and build new garden beds. And while there's still mulching and pruning, and some sowing and planting to do; winter jobs can usually wait. If conditions don't suit working outside, go in and read books or listen to true crime podcasts with a clear conscious. Possibly you can even put some time into planning for the gardening year ahead that will pay off next winter, that seems to have a certain natural logic to it.

And while there may not be as much to harvest, winter makes what you can pick and eat seem a sweeter reward. Literally so, parsnips, yams, swedes and turnips, even kale, Brussels sprouts and broccoli, have a higher sugar-to-starch ratio over cold winters – sugar is a natural anti-freeze that protects them from frost damage, so they all taste sweeter after a frost. I don't know if that's a metaphor or just interesting horticultural trivia. Maybe it's both?

Softneck garlic usually does not send up a scape or a flower stem; and hardneck garlic usually does. If you want to make garlic braids for easier storage, or for the aesthetic, grow a softneck.

Garlic

The thing everyone knows about garlic is you plant it on the shortest day and harvest it on the longest, which (ironically) is not especially useful or even true for most of the garlic you can grow in New Zealand. That rule treats garlic like it's all the same and actually, garlic is divided into two sub-species, hardneck and softneck, and those two subspecies are divided into 10 groups (actually 11, but only 10 are available in New Zealand). Softneck garlics include silverskin and artichoke; while hardneck garlics include turban, creole, Asiatic, porcelain, rocambole, standard purple stripe, marbled purple stripe and glazed purple stripe. All those garlic groups have different winter chill requirements, different storage life, different flavour profiles and different optimal planting and harvesting times: you might be planting anytime between March and June and harvesting between November and February.

It's worth trying to find a garlic variety that does well where you live, especially if you find one less prone to garlic rust in your region, a fungal disease that has been a problem across New Zealand for a few years. But if you want anything other than softneck silverskin and artichoke garlic varieties (both of which are commercially grown: 'Printanor', the most commonly available seed garlic you find for sale in New Zealand, is a silverskin) then you have to hunt around for it. It's usually only available at specialty nurseries and they sell out indecently quickly. Gary Patterson, who grows all 10 different garlic groups on the shores of Lake Wakatipu (and sells them as Gourmet Garlic), told me he sold his entire year's stock in less than 24 hours last year. So find specialist garlic growers, sign up for their newsletters and follow their socials so you know when stock goes on sale. Look for growers south of you and at a higher altitude: Gary told me garlic acclimatises best when the seed bulbs have come from a colder climate to a warmer one and from a higher altitude, of 300m-plus, to a lower one (garlic seed cloves grown in the north and planted in the south are likely to produce only miniature bulbs for the first few years while they acclimatise).

Garlic needs vernalisation, or exposure to cold, for the bulb to form (without it, plants don't form bulbs but single clove bulbs called rounds). The vernalisation required varies between the groups but ideally, you want a month or two at 5-10°C. In a cold winter, you get that planting them outside, but in warmer regions Gary says you can artificially vernalise bulbs by popping them in the warmest part of the fridge for 2-3 weeks before you plant. Plant cloves on the day you crack them from the bulb, as soon as they are separated hibernation ceases.

And garlic rust? The Australian Garlic Industry Association claims that one factor needed for garlic rust to develop is that the leaves stayed wet for at least four hours. A grower told me growing undercover, in a tunnelhouse or under a row cover, to keep it dry, can keep it rust-free.

Broccoli

I love broccoli, it's probably my favourite vegetable. But it's not without its challenges to grow, I have to admit. It's necessary to get it in the ground early enough so that it is warm enough for the plants to grow a decent-sized root system to keep growing (slowly) over winter. I find the bigger varieties have to be in the ground at the start of autumn in my Auckland garden; you probably want to plant them in late summer down south. That means you need to start seed in summer when winter brassicas are the last thing on your mind, but this is a crop that you need to plan ahead for. If you leave it too late and it's too cold, they just sulk in the ground and do nothing until spring. But that means you're juggling with the fact that if it's warm enough for the plants to grow that usually means it's warm enough for white butterfly – and the white butterfly caterpillars will devour broccoli at the first opportunity. So you need to protect your broccoli with nets or a row cover. I do like the mini varieties like 'Green Mini' or 'Mighty Mini', they are quicker to grow, take up less space and – crucially – are much easier to net or cover. But my real favourite is sprouting broccoli. Plant seedlings as per regular broccoli and wait: they do nothing much for ages and you need to protect them from cabbage whites if they are about. But by spring they are huge plants that produce in abundance and the more you pick the more of the sweet purple stems are produced. I always have to pull them out before they stop producing to make way for other things but I've heard from gardeners who have it producing for six months or more. Bart Acres in Dunedin told me sprouting purple broccoli is one of his favourite winter crops: he sows in January and plants seedlings in February and harvests all through winter, picking purple florets every few days. He told me the younger leaves are sweet and tender and can be used like kale too.

The best crop of broccoli I ever grew was under BHU horticultural mesh row cover (see page 137), I think the extra warmth that provided made a huge difference to its winter growth.

Cabbages **thriving** in the Matakana community garden.

Cabbages

I don't grow cabbages every year. I find them less useful than broccoli and they take a long time: four months-plus from seed. When I do grow them from seed, I sow them in trays in late summer to plant out early to mid-autumn. In colder regions I'd sow in midsummer to plant in early autumn. But this is one crop I more often buy as a seedling rather than sow: I don't have the space to grow many, plus a packet of open-pollinated cabbage seeds might contain 200 seeds or more and frankly, the thought of having to get through 200 cabbages over the rest of my natural span makes me feel a little depressed. Cabbages – in fact all brassicas – hate to dry out so I usually puddle the seedlings in: dig the hole, fill it with water and wait for it to drain, then plant the seedling, backfill and water again. Like broccoli, it's a juggle, you want the seedlings in early enough to get established in warm soil, but that means you need to protect them as long as the cabbage whites are about (in fact you can grow cabbage all year round, but I have never bothered trying over summer, it would be a 24-hour job guarding them from cabbage whites). I do like what are called Chinese cabbages, which is a loose term that can mean a few different hearting brassicas that are sometimes classed as Asian greens: wong bok is the one you see most often. I find them much quicker growing, ready about six weeks or so after planting, and you can use it in place of traditional cabbage but they don't have that distinctive 'brassica' taste, and I do mean that pejoratively.

All brassicas appreciate growing in firm soil. You don't want to compact the soil but compress it: patting it down hard before you plant, or even going heel to toe across it, and heeling in seedlings firmly after planting. Earth up the stem as it grows too to keep it secure. Brassicas, as a genus, hate wind rock and will produce only small heads if grown in loose soil.

Kate's Asian coleslaw

This is another recipe from my sister Kate, who was trying to make a coleslaw with a dressing that was zingy rather than creamy. This dressing is delicious, it's worth making a double lot and using it on other salads.

For the salad use a mix of finely sliced red cabbage and green cabbage. I probably use twice as much red to green just for the look, but use whatever you grew. Grab a couple of carrots, scrub them and grate them and throw them in. Add chopped spring onion if you have it, or half a finely sliced red onion instead. Sometimes I throw in a couple of finely sliced chillies as well. Finally, add a good cupful of chopped mint and coriander. To make the dressing: add the juice of two lemons, a couple of tablespoons each of brown sugar and sweet chilli sauce, a quarter of a cup of soy sauce and a teaspoon of sesame oil to a jar and shake well. Dress the coleslaw, toss, and add a generous amount of chopped roasted salted peanuts.

Cauliflower cranberry salad

This is another recipe from Kate, although she was given it by her mother-in-law Lynda Macdonald who herself had it passed on to her by a pensioner at the supermarket over the cauliflower display. She had to rush home to write it down. Lynda admits she might not have recalled it verbatim but either way, this version is excellent.

Add about 5 or 6 cups of cauliflower cut into small florets (or a mix of cauliflower and broccoli is fine) to a bowl along with ½ cup of dried cranberries, ½ cup of silvered almonds, and 1 cup of finely sliced celery.

Make the dressing by mixing ½ cup of olive oil, ¼ cup each of red wine vinegar and maple syrup with ½ teaspoon each of ground allspice and salt. Pour the dressing on the salad and mix. It tastes better if you let it stand for 30 minutes or so before serving.

Bougie cob loaf spinach dip

You often see it suggested, indeed I have suggested it myself over the years, that in your vegetable garden you should grow only what you and your family like to eat. But I increasingly wonder if we have that the right way round. If there's something you can grow easily and in abundance, try to find a way to make it taste delicious.

Take this recipe, which comes from my good friend and one-time flatmate Tennille Bergin. It is ridiculously easy and outrageously delicious: I guarantee it will convert even the most ardent anti-spinach eater or silverbeet skeptic.

Start with one of those round sourdough loaves and hollow it out, tearing up the bread you pull out of the middle so you have little bits of bread for dipping. Then you mix a tub of sour cream, a tub of cream cheese, a decent amount of spinach or silverbeet (or both) that you have blanched, squeezed and chopped and one packet of French onion soup (I also throw in some kale if I have a lot of it although if you do that, remove the central stem from each leaf). You put all that in the hollowed-out bread and bake for 20 or so minutes at 160°C, with all the little dipping bits on the oven tray around the outside to crisp up. Tennille says if you are making it for a party, you can add chopped chives or spring onion or even sprinkle crispy pieces of bacon or prosciutto on top and serve it with vegetable crudites to try and disguise its basic bougie nature.

Kate's Asian
coleslaw

Clockwise from top left: Cauliflower; 'Romanesco' cauliflower, sometimes called 'Romanesco' broccoli; planting celery seedlings; Brussels sprout plants.

Cauliflower

I find cauliflowers to be the most temperamental of the brassicas. As with their cruciferous cousins, you want them in while the soil is warm enough that they can get established, they are more cold-tender than cabbage. I have heard from gardeners down south that immature plants can be wiped out by a frost so you can instead plant seedlings in spring, after the risk of frost has passed, but if it gets too hot (and cauliflower is a long game, the bigger varieties can take three months from planting), then the caulis will bolt immediately to seed (or button, which means the heads are small or irregular). But it is worth growing the spectacularly beautiful 'Romanesco' (sometimes called Romanesco broccoli although it's actually not broccoli, or even a cauliflower although it is usually lumped in with caulis). Romanesco is truly a work of art, had M.C. Escher gone in for plant breeding. The florets form natural fractals, or a pattern that looks the same on any scale, and that pattern is a repeating spiral, which is itself an example of a Fibonacci sequence, where each number is the sum of the two previous numbers. It's so beautiful, it will take your breath away. Just to warn you when you cook it and eat it, it still just tastes like a nuttier cauliflower.

Brussels sprouts

Brussels sprouts do better if you get a frost. I love them but don't grow them in Auckland. I have tried, and they form loose rosettes rather than the tight heads they produce in colder climates. But if you have the right conditions (cool summer, properly cold winter), plant prior to Christmas if you want to harvest over winter or in autumn to harvest in spring. If you grow them, pick sprouts from the bottom first and work your way up, they will continue producing sprouts from the top.

Celery

Celery needs moisture. It doesn't like sitting in wet soil, more you need to keep the water supply up. It was originally a bog plant. The wettest autumn and winter I have ever lived through saw my best-ever celery crop. I plant it as a seedling in early autumn, you might plant as early as midsummer in southern regions provided you can give it the constant access to water that it requires.

Cutting celery, also called leaf celery, celery for cutting, and par-cel, is a dwarf celery that looks like flat-leaf parsley but tastes like celery and can be used in place of celery in recipes. It's good in pots, needs less water and I personally find it much easier to grow than celery proper.

Leeks

Leeks are, like garlic, an edible allium. They are absolute slow-pokes: and most people who complain to me they can't grow them are simply not giving them enough time. If I am starting from seed, I start in trays in spring: they are slow to germinate and the seedlings are also easy to miss, as wispy as grass. You can grow them on in trays for a couple of months until they have more presence and get them in the ground while the soil is still warm so they can establish before winter: you can also plant them in early autumn in warmer regions and frankly you are better to do so north of Auckland, since if you start in spring the increasing day length can trigger them to bolt. When you plant leeks, you want to give them room to fatten up, so use the handle of your rake or a dibber to make deep, straight holes, drop a seedling into each one and backfill, so only the top few centimetres are above the soil line. You can mound as they grow to keep more of the base of the leek white but I don't usually bother: the green part is still edible. Plant and wait: they take months. If everything goes wrong and they never fatten up, just use them as spring onions and call it a win.

Onions

Another edible allium, onions are, like garlic, a complicated and diverse family and different members require different growing conditions. I strongly urge you if you are starting out to begin with onions sets rather than seed or even seedlings, sets are far easier and less fussy. Basically, they are immature onions you plant like a bulb. You plant them in spring and harvest them when the leaves start to yellow off and fall over.

Parsnips

The big thing with parsnips is to sow absolutely fresh seed direct in spring (or again in early autumn in warmer regions) and keep it continuously moist while it germinates. A lot of gardeners cover newly sown seed with a plank or a piece of hessian or something until the seedlings appear to keep water in the soil (see page 67). I know a lot of successful parsnip growers who also swear by first digging a trench for parsnips, then boiling the jug and pouring the boiling water along the trench. When it stops steaming, sow your seeds. But even then, parsnips are a boogieman crop for a lot of gardeners. Because germination is patchy, I usually sow three seeds together. In the event they all grow – and they don't always for me – discard the two weaker-growing seedlings.

Shallots are definitely worth growing. I find them easier than onions and I use them in place of onions quite often. Plant from late autumn until early spring. When you plant, leave about half the bulb above the soil and harvest after the leaves have gone brown and begun to die back.

Clockwise from top left: Plant leeks by making a planting hole with a dibber or a piece of dowel; leeks; freshly harvested parsnips; onions.

Caitlin Huynh's patio garden in Auckland is 3.5m by 4m. But she grows a range of veges, herbs and fruit in containers here. "We don't need to buy a lot of veges," she told me.

Small spaces

It's perfectly possible to produce abundant veges on bijou sections and balconies, and actually for beginners, lack of space is no bad thing.

A common reason people give me as to why they don't grow food is they don't have space.

t is probably the most common reason actually, or maybe an equal first with people who say they don't have the time (see page 20). Now obviously there are a lot of variables but if you were to ask, how much space would I need to grow fresh food; I would say, not much. Almost certainly not as much as you think.

You could produce an abundance of herbs and leafy greens in just a few containers and pots in a courtyard, or on a balcony if you are in an apartment. You can use any suitable wall space to grow climbing beans or peas or train the smaller-fruiting cucurbits (cucumbers, little pumpkins and watermelons, zucchini) to grow up rather than sprawl out.

Don't have a balcony or courtyard? Well, there are plenty of edible crops you can grow on a windowsill: try microgreens, herbs, salad crops and leafy things, and suitable sorts of tomatoes. My mother Rosaleen, in Hamilton, grows 'Tumbling Tom' tomatoes in two hanging baskets on the balcony every year, one red and one yellow.

I even grow food inside my house. In my kitchen I have a little plug-in Vegepod Kitchen Garden, which has an integrated LED grow light to keep everything growing. It does take up some bench space (mine is 60cm by 22cm) but the salads crops in it grow, by my estimation, about twice as fast as the ones outside, plus they are immediately at hand when I am cooking.

In fact, I am going to go out on a limb and say if you are new to gardening, lack confidence about your ability to keep plants alive or are in any way concerned about having enough time to look after a garden – or any combination of those three – then a lack of space is actually an advantage.

Obviously, a small space is less work and less money, both to set up and to maintain. But, perhaps more importantly, it's also far easier to see what's happening in a small garden and so keep ahead of problems, especially because it's likely to be close to, or even part of, your living space.

You are more likely, or at least I am, to eat what you grow when it's handy. Even in my small-ish garden I rarely fancy going right down to the bottom of it to pick something when it's cold, dark, raining or all three.

But also growing edible crops in a space that you can easily see and often pass through or spend time in means you spot and address problems more quickly, and it's much easier to keep on top of basic stuff like watering. Frankly about 80 percent of success in the vegetable garden comes down to, basically, keeping an eye on things, and small spaces make that vastly easier to do.

Clockwise from top left: Wood trellis in Caitlin Huynh's Auckland garden; she harvested 4kg of spuds from two grow bags; the garden in spring; as well as Spencer the dog, the space is home to Kitty the cat.

You can define the grid in square-metre gardening. I don't usually myself, but it's not a bad idea as it means you can see immediately when a square is empty.

Square-metre gardening

In small spaces – I mean in all spaces but especially in small spaces – you want to make sure you are producing the maximum amount of food in the space you have. There are various ways you can grow food more intensively but the one I use is the technique known as either square-metre gardening or square-foot gardening if you are of an imperial or American persuasion. It's basically an intensive growing method where you plant crops in clumps in a grid, rather than in rows, which uses space more effectively.

There's an American gardening book by retired engineer Mel Bartholomew, *Square Foot Gardening,* which came out in 1981 and really popularised the name for this method, although you could argue it's a system that's been around for hundreds of years. But Bartholomew's much reprinted book is still worth a read, although I personally prefer Australian gardening writer Lolo Houbein's updated approach (read her 2007 book *One Magic Square*), as her system allows a lot more design flexibility and if you get bored of grids you can do spirals and mandalas.

The basic principle of the OG method though is you grow your edible crops in a square bed and that square is divided up into smaller spaces, like the smaller squares on a chess board. So, if you have a 1m square bed, you can divide that up into 16 growing cells that are 25cm by 25cm. My beds are 1.5m, so the squares are bigger, but I just apply the same principle. You can create the grid on top of the soil using twine, stakes, or dowel to define the different cells. In each cell you closely plant your veges; either one, four, nine or 16 plants per square and that number depends on the plant's overall size at maturity and speed of growth.

Here's the plan I made for one of the beds at my place a few years ago. In the top northwest corner, I planted the perennial New Zealand spinach; in the next square, four bok choy; next to that chives; and in the top northeast corner, one cucumber (while I was waiting for it to be warm enough to plant a cucumber, I used the space for microgreens).

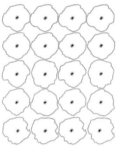

Square Spacing - 20 plants

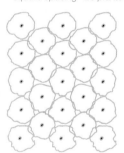

Hexagonal Spacing - 23 plants

In his iconic book *How to Grow More Vegetables,* John Jeavons makes the point that when spacing vegetables, a diagonally offset or hexagonal spacing pattern – so you stagger each row back and forth – is a more efficient way to use the space than a simple grid. You can grow about 10 to 15 percent more seedlings in it while still allowing the same amount of space between them.

In the next two rows down, I sowed eight different sorts of lettuce (you can usually get four lettuces to one square although sometimes I only plant two if it's a bigger variety). In the bottom row on the southwest corner I grew more rocket (I just sprinkle a spoonful of seed on the soil), in the next square 20-25 radishes from seed; next to that sorrel; and in the bottom southeast corner, one tomato (again, I used the space for microgreens until it was warm enough to plant tomatoes). Whatever you grow, keep tall plants on the south side to avoid shading the small plants.

There's a lot to like about this method. Plants are so closely planted they form a living mulch, which reduces weeding – something I hate doing. Because you are continually harvesting and planting, there's a natural crop rotation taking place, which helps prevent plant-specific pests and diseases building up. It keeps the workload manageable, as you never have that much to do on any one day, and it helps avoid gluts of a lot of something ready to eat all at once.

But it works best if you are someone who spends time in the garden pretty regularly. It suits someone who does a little bit fairly often rather than someone who likes to fling a heap of crops in on Labour Weekend and just see what survives. Any intensively planted crops take up water quickly, so you need to keep a careful eye on irrigation and in summer, you'll probably need to be prepared to water every day. The soil mix you grow in is absolutely key too, with so many crops growing in it the soil needs to be extremely rich in organic matter, friable and perfectly free-draining. Mel Bartholomew recommended using something he called Mel's mix, which was equal parts peat, vermiculite and compost. Obviously, now you'd want to avoid highly unsustainable peat, but I have substituted one part coconut coir and also just used two parts compost to one part vermiculite (although the second option does dry out a lot faster) and both worked fine.

True believers claim you can grow anything in this system, but my experience is it better suits smaller plants with a relatively compact habit (such as lettuces and herbs) or which can be trained vertically (like well-staked tomatoes or cucurbits trained up a trellis). I don't use it to grow bulky crops like potatoes or onions, or crops that both grow slowly and take up space, such as brassicas.

Usually with square-metre gardening, you are growing in a raised bed. If you don't have raised beds, you could apply the idea to a ground-level plot but it's crucial to have that great drainage and exceptional growing mix, and that's much easier to control in a raised bed than in the ground.

If you don't have space for a 1m bed, you can create about a square metre of growing space using around six or seven pots with a 40cm diameter. Group them closely together, and treat each one as an individual cell or double cell.

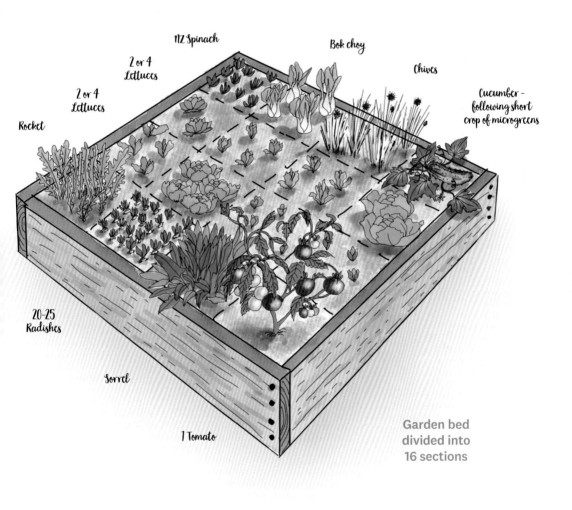

1.5m x 1.5m Garden Bed
Taller plants on southern side of garden bed to prevent shading of remaining quadrants

NZ Spinach

Bok choy

2 or 4 Lettuces

Chives

2 or 4 Lettuces

Cucumber – following short crop of microgreens

Rocket

20-25 Radishes

Sorrel

1 Tomato

Garden bed divided into 16 sections

Interestingly, one of the most revolutionary aspects of square-foot gardening when Mel Bartholomew's book first came out was the suggestion not to walk on, or dig, your soil.

The pros and cons of Vegepods

Vegepod, if you don't already know, is a brand that was started in Australia, which puts out a range of kitset gardening products but they are best known for the enclosed self-watering container gardening systems they sell, which are called Vegepods.

Now Vegepods are quite spendy to buy and when they were first released in New Zealand in 2016 I was a bit sneery about them and probably cast the odd nasturtium along the lines of the people who bought them simply not realising that vegetables could also grow in the ground. But then my older sister Jane was given one and loved it and grew lots in it. And the more I poked around in her one, the more I liked it. So now I think that while there is a significant initial investment involved, they are a clever system that sidesteps a lot of the problems that gardeners, especially new gardeners, have.

PROS

So first the pros: the number-one reason I like them is that they are self-watering or wicking. Wicking is essentially a passive form of hydroponics: the soil inside the pod is held above a water reservoir and the soil or perlite that is in contact with outlet holes of that water reservoir acts like a wick and draws the water up into the soil for your plants when it is needed (exactly like a wick draws up kerosene in an old-timey lamp). Provided there's water in the reservoir of course, but the standard cover is permeable so rain travels through the soil to refill the reservoir and if it's not raining at all and/or very hot you can add water yourself. I love wicking systems: they prevent both underwatering and overwatering (both of which cause problems) and moreover they provide water to your vege crops consistently, which is both more important and harder to do than you might think. (You can build wicking beds yourself if you don't have enough jingle to shell out for a Vegepod, see the instructions on page 94).

I actually think Vegepods are a great way to produce fresh food in a small space, especially if your main focus is cut-and-come-again leafy greens and herbs. I love the fact they are self-watering and avoid or at least minimise a lot of potential pest problems if you use them right. They are a great choice for new gardeners or if you lack confidence and/or time, but also for renters and apartment-dwellers: I often see them on apartment balconies in downtown Auckland. Yes, they cost a bit but they are one of the easiest, most fool-proof ways to grow veges that I have seen.

Lisa and Andy Lowe, who set
up Vegepod in New Zealand,
with their dog Chase.

The second big pro for me is the cover of the pod itself. The outdoor pods have a flip cover that opens up, like the lid on a sushi box, when you need to plant, harvest or water but which you can (and in fact should according to Vegepod best practice) leave shut the rest of the time. And that cover provides a physical barrier that will keep out some – not all, but most – pests. Slugs, snails, white cabbage butterflies, various caterpillars and bugs, birds, cats, dogs, rats, mice: none of them can get through a closed cover to infest, eat or otherwise destroy your growing crops. Plus, that cover also creates a microclimate, which means things will grow faster and you can start heat-loving crops sooner and grow them longer. Lisa Lowe, who set up the New Zealand arm of the business with her husband Andy, told me she grows basil year-round in her outdoor Vegepod in Tauranga, for instance.

CONS

But there are, if not quite cons, perhaps limitations to this system too. You can probably already see that if pests should make their way into the pod – stowing away on new seedlings or seizing the opportunity when you have the lid open, say – they will absolutely love it there and start large, multigenerational families. And no wonder, it's lovely and warm, there's lots to eat, and they are protected from their own natural predators. The mesh is also not fine enough to stop really small pests: Lisa told me some customers have had aphids make their way through, in which case I'd assume tomato-potato psyllid could get in on to your tomatoes too because they are about the same size.

This system also suits some kinds of crops and is less suitable for growing others. Lisa says she finds the easiest and most successful crops to grow in them are leafy greens. "Spinach, lettuces, kale, silverbeet, Asian greens, celery, leafy herbs, those are what I grow".

But the cover only gives you about 70cm of growing height above the soil so obviously the system doesn't suit very tall crops like corn. Lisa says she hears from lots of gardeners who grow fruiting plants, like tomatoes, eggplants, capsicums and chillies, in their pods very

On the bench: This is a Vegepod product Kitchen Garden on my bench. It's the same principle as the outdoor pods: a soil bed held above a water reservoir so the water wicks into the soil with the addition of a grow light on a timer. I'll admit when I was gifted it by Vegepod I thought it was very silly but now I have given it a grow, I think it's fun. They are spendy to buy and it would take you a while to recoup the cost in terms of harvests... but given the cost of fruit and vegetables you would eventually! I am growing salad things in mine at the moment but in spring I am going to try and use it to strike cuttings. The knitted sushi on the wall was made by my sister Kate.

I like the system but it best suits salad leaves, herbs and other leafy crops.

Clockwise from top left: Belinda Stone in Feilding, Manawatu, demonstrating how the string holds the lid up; Caitlin Te Tai in Khandallah, Wellington; Lisa Robinson in Foxton; Amanda Clark in Palmerston North.

successfully: in fact those heat-lovers love the warmth and appreciate the constant access to moisture. But Lisa says you do need to choose the variety that you grow carefully – look for varieties of those plants that have container, dwarf or patio in the variety name and/or are described as suitable for pots – otherwise they can get too big. She has seen customers growing bigger fruiting plants, like beefsteak tomatoes which easily get to 2m tall in my outside garden, but it does require training of the fruiting stems to grow horizontally. Likewise, runner beans and peas can be grown in a pod, Lisa says, but need to be trained along horizontal supports: it's probably easier to focus on lower-growing bush beans. Brassicas like broccoli, cabbages and cauliflowers can be grown in one but they do take up a lot of the available space and for a long time since they grow slowly. Large scrambling vining plants like cucumbers, melons, pumpkins or zucchini can be grown too, again they love the heat and constant access to water. But they do tend to overwhelm the available growing space pretty quickly, so Lisa says some customers plant those crops inside and train them, so the vines grow outside the pod. "But then of course you can't shut the cover properly and there are downsides to that".

And since there's only 30cm of soil depth, the system isn't suitable for bigger root crops like potatoes or kūmara. You could grow smaller root crops, like radishes, carrots and beetroot but be aware if you have used a premium vege-growing mix to fill your pod, it is quite likely to contain a nitrogen-rich, controlled-release fertiliser that won't suit root vegetables (nitrogen feeds leafy growth so you'll end up with all leafy top and little or no edible root).

Finally, if you want ongoing success with your Vegepod, you need to put time and energy into the soil (that's also a fundamental truth worth remembering for anything you grow in pots, and indeed the wider garden and wider world). Lisa highly recommends adding a layer of a couple of inches of perlite before you fill the pod, which is a soil additive made of a naturally occurring siliceous rock, which helps improve drainage, aeration and water retention. It's great as a layer between the soil and the water reservoir as it stops the soil seeping into the water reservoir "and it wicks the water up even better than soil". It's incredibly light too, much lighter than soil, so using it makes the Vegepod a bit easier to move around if you want to be able to do that. Then on top of the perlite use a good-quality bagged potting mix (go for the best you can afford, you really do get what you pay for, see page 245). You want a pathogen- and weed-free mix that contains a controlled-release fertiliser, water crystals or a wetting agent, possibly a fungicide. And of course, what you grow will take up some of what is in that original mix, so you need to keep feeding the soil in between crops. Lisa says she gets asked quite often if you need to take all the soil out between crops and put new soil in. And you don't, she assures me. "But every three or four months, or in between crops, dig the mix over to keep it aerated and add whatever you want to use to feed your soil, maybe seaweed solution, liquid fertiliser, worm casings or compost".

As well as that, I'd use liquid fertilisers every few weeks over the growing season. I tend to prefer liquid fertilisers for containers. I think it's too easy to overdo it with granular fertiliser in pots, even with natural fertiliser it's easy to over-apply.

For non-stop crops, leave no bare soil. You want plants to be just touching at maturity but not overlapping.

Succession
planting explained

Succession planting is taking a staggered approach to growing veges, which means – in theory, at least – you have a consistent supply of crops ready to eat. In small spaces it's a method that lets you squeeze more edible harvests out of the growing space that you have. So I try to sow or plant a few lettuces every two weeks so we always have fresh lettuces to replace the ones we are eating. Some stuff you might not plant every couple of weeks but you can get more from the space by judicious replanting once or twice: I put in new zucchini, cucumbers and bush beans in December or January which will be producing about when the ones I planted in late October start to get tatty and slow down. The key to success with succession is organisation: you need to have seedlings on standby ready to go as soon as you have gaps. You can sow seed to fill gaps too of course, but for maximum efficient use of growing space you are better buying seedlings or starting crops in trays and having seedlings ready to transplant. When you transplant you save the time the seedlings have already spent growing: say, you start beans in a seed tray and in a couple of weeks they are big enough to shift into the garden, but for that two weeks you've been using that space to grow something else. But whether you are planting or sowing to make the optimal use of the growing space, replant or resow as quickly as possible, definitely a day or two. Although never rush to pull out what could produce again. Yotam and Niva Kay, who run the market garden Pakaraka Permaculture in Thames, and grow a staggering amount of food on the land they have (about 12,000kg a year on a third of an acre) told me they think the very best way to increase yield from the available space is by getting another crop from anything cut-and-come-again (which includes lots of leafy green crops). When you harvest, cut the leaves off with scissors about 3cm above soil level (see page 90). Leave the roots in the soil, show the plant some love with compost and liquid fertiliser, and then, hopefully, you'll get another harvest from it.

Intercropping

I class intercropping, where you effectively plant fast-growing vegetables in the same space as you are growing slower-growing vegetables, as a kind of succession planting: so you might sow or plant speedy rocket, lettuce, radishes or spinach in between rows of brassicas or sweetcorn. By the time those slower-growing crops get big enough to grow into or shade out the space that the faster ones are in, you will have harvested the speedsters. The faster-growing crop provides an additional benefit too, as a temporary living mulch covering your soil while you wait for the slower crops to get big enough to need that space.

Use your vertical spaces

You can use walls, fences and even posts to create extra growing spaces in small gardens. Add trellis or rebar to support climbers like runner beans, peas and passionfruit. Most cucurbits – that's cucumbers, zucchini, squash, pumpkins and melons – will climb too if you give them the opportunity to do so. You might need to encourage them a bit at first weaving them into the support or tying them on with something soft and stretchy.

With the last three especially, only grow the smaller-fruiting varieties if you want them to climb, otherwise the heavy fruit will pull the vine straight off the support. And even then, once the fruit sets, create little individual hammocks that you can tie on to the trellis or support to take the weight off the vine. You can use those net bags that onions come in, old laddered tights, I have even seen old bras repurposed as good gourd support.

There are a lot of wall-mounted vertical gardening systems you can buy and use to grow shallow-rooted salad greens, herbs and strawberries. I am on the fence (jk!) about these vertical gardening systems myself. I have seen some good-but-expensive options for sale that offer a decent soil depth for each plant and some kind of integrated irrigation system. But there are also lots of cheaper options that offer very shallow soil depth for each plant and no irrigation. With these it's very hard – I would say impossible – to get the irrigation right. With so little soil around the plants' roots to hold water, and extra exposure to the drying effect of wind because they are vertical, they dry out incredibly fast. Plus it's hard to water everything growing in them evenly, as most of the water can end up trickling down to the plants at the bottom.

For the same reason I don't really rate those DIY gardens people make from old pallets or from lengths of guttering suspended horizontally on a wall for growing veges: I don't believe that either option really offers enough soil depth for most edible plants to thrive.

I have had better results at my place using my vertical spaces to grow plants in individual terracotta pots that are hung on the wall by Leylandlatches. These are a great New Zealand-designed resin plant pot hanger that fit any standard terracotta pot between 9cm and 21cm, you just screw them directly to the wall. Pots give a much better soil depth for each plant than some of the cheaper vertical systems, and the greater the soil volume the greater its moisture-holding capacity, so they don't dry out quite as fast.

Clockwise from top left: Go vertical with obelisks; and trellis; Leylandlatches; gourd support.

Pots & containers

It's easy to grow veges in
pots, tubs, buckets, hanging
baskets, even cardboard boxes.
Plus it's perfect for beginners,
balcony gardeners and renters.

I grow lots of edibles in pots at my place and there's a lot to recommend it, I reckon.

Growing in pots is a great way to start your first vege garden. It keeps things contained (jk!), as in you can start small and grow a bit and build up as your skills and confidence grow. It's highly likely setting up pots is going to be faster and cheaper than setting up garden beds or creating new growing spaces; plus, pots are by their nature temporary so you can grow almost anything in them while you spend some time working out the perfect spot for an in-ground vege garden or permanent raised beds and setting them up.

Plus, with pots, it doesn't matter what your garden soil is like. The soil in my garden in Auckland is heavy volcanic clay. I've been amending it over the last 15 or so years, and I'm making progress, but improving soil is not what you'd call fast work. Or say you have no soil and want to grow food on a balcony or in a concreted courtyard. No problem, just gather suitable containers, fill them with a decent potting mix and get planting.

Growing in pots helps me keep track of things that go dormant in the winter (like horseradish or chives), and it contains the colonising ways of borderline invasive plants (like mint or, again, horseradish). Containing or limiting the size of the root ball limits the eventual size of some plants too: so, it keeps my bay and makrut lime to a handy and harvestable-from size.

And an obvious advantage of pots is they are movable. I have a brick house and so in the winter I tuck a lemon tree that I have in a pot at the base of a north-facing wall: the wall acts like a heat sink, catching the sun all day and that warmth is gradually released at night. If I'm going away in the summer, I move plants in pots into shade or semi-shade to slow down the rate at which plants take up and use water. I also have herbs and salad things in pots right at the back door, so they are handy when I am cooking, and I don't have to go right down into the garden if it's dark or raining or both.

Now I would say that I reckon success growing in pots is a bit trickier than growing in the ground. I was talking to Paul Wylaars who's a manager at Zealandia Horticulture Ltd, which is one of New Zealand's largest suppliers of seedlings and plants, about this the other day and he pointed out that a plant in the ground can put out such a big root structure and that just makes them more resilient; whereas with a plant in a pot, it's obviously limited in the resources it can call on. For the same reason you also are likely to get a lower yield from a plant in a pot than a plant growing under the same conditions in the ground.

But if the soil, water and plant choice is right you pump out food in pots and I highly recommend giving them a grow.

Garden designer
Joanna Hamilton and
her husband Mark have
lived in an Auckland
apartment for more
than 12 years now, but
still grow a range of
veges, herbs and citrus.

Another view of the potager in pots on the balcony of Joanna and Mark Hamilton's Auckland apartment. I visited it during Garden DesignFest one year, it is just amazing.

What pots can you grow in?

Pretty much anything you can put soil in, that has drainage holes and won't leach anything toxic into the soil, can be used as a container in which to grow veges. I used to upcycle old plastic containers like milk bottles and ice cream containers quite a bit in my garden – they are tough and retain water well, plus they are light enough that you can still lift them even when full of soil. But I tend to avoid using them now: while, according to what I have read, food-grade plastic (as in, anything that has had food in it) is also safe to grow food in, I find some of those plastic containers break down very fast when exposed to sunlight. I still re-use plastic plant pots although I try and avoid buying more, and I'd be fine to grow something in an old bucket with drainage holes. I have used those double cardboard boxes that meal kit deliveries come in to grow potatoes, they did break down eventually, but it took a few months, by which time we had eaten all the potatoes. Those white polystyrene boxes that you see fruit and vegetables packed into are good too: lightweight and easy to move around. They can be fragile, so handle them carefully, but I have had them last for years. They are also shallow, so don't give you much soil depth, but they have a lot of surface area so you can pack a lot of shallow-rooted lettuces and salad leaves in them, just sow seed thickly on the top. Any kind of terracotta or ceramic container that has drainage holes is fine, but you will need to use a sealant spray on the inside of terracotta pots, or they will lose water too quickly. Wooden crates are great although look for ones where there isn't too much of a gap between the slats on the sides: I have tried to use beer crates in the past and lined them with hessian which I thought would look rustic and cool and stop the soil from spilling out the wide gaps between the slats. But when I filled the crate with potting mix the hessian bulged out of the gaps. It probably still would have been fine to grow in, but I could not look at it without being triggered into flashbacks of when I found an old pair of jeans from a few years ago and tried, optimistically, to put them on.

Fun fact: some plants like having their roots contained and so do better, relatively, in pots than in the ground. Figs, for instance, will fruit more for the size they are if they are grown in a container. I grow one in a half-wine barrel at my place. That also keeps the tree small and easy to pick from. In the soil, they grow gigantic and birds are the only ones that get any figs.

What about growing in tyres?

Look, it's going to be controversial I know but I don't do this myself or recommend it. You see it suggested as an option all the time: the point is made that old tyres are an easy-to-get waste material and using them in the garden keeps them out of landfill; they can be stacked to create retaining walls with integrated growing space or upcycled into a compost system; they retain water well plus the black rubber heats up in the sun and releases that heat gradually at night so they effectively function as heat sinks. And all of that is absolutely true, but I still wouldn't want to eat anything grown in them. I heard a scientist from Plant & Food Research talking about this a few years ago and he said that tyres are made of a range of materials including heavy metals and some known carcinogens, and while it is fair to say the rate and extent to which those leach into the soil is not consistent nor completely understood, even if you aren't concerned about that you have to consider the various contaminants and emissions on the road surface that would have been picked while the tyre was in use. There are lots of things you can grow veges in – many free and freely available – I say give tyres a swerve.

How big should pots be?

It does depend on what you are growing a bit, but in general the bigger the better. If you are growing veges look for pots that are 30-40cm deep and don't go for anything any smaller than a bucket. With shallow-rooted salad-y things like lettuces, mesclun mix, mizuna, mibuna and mustard you can get away with something shallower, especially if you want to harvest it as a baby leaf, but I would still look for at least 20cm of soil depth. Soil holds water and the less soil your pot contains the quicker it will dry out; plus, soil contains the nutrients that plants need. Of course, soil is also very heavy, so a big pot full of soil is difficult to move around. But if you want to move your pots often, rather than going for smaller pots I'd suggest investing in plant pots that have wheels on, or banging up a DIY version of the same if you are that way inclined. You can also buy separate wheeled casters or wheeled trays or plant saucers that you can put under your pots before you fill them. These can be absolutely great, but I have also bought cheaper ones that collapse on first use. I'd suggest buying the best quality you can afford and keeping (well) under the suggested weight limit.

Do pots need saucers? Yes and no. Saucers are useful over summer, they stop plants drying out too quickly, and of course they project the surface the pot stands on. But over winter I put pots on feet or bricks to improve drainage so plants aren't constantly sitting in water.

Don't fill pots with pure compost. If you read British gardening magazines and books, they often talk about planting in compost. But in the UK people seem to refer to what in New Zealand we would call potting mix as compost or potting compost. What we call compost is just decomposed organic matter, and not suitable for growing in all by itself.

Best soil for veges in pots

I cannot stress enough how important soil is for crops in pots. Don't fill pots with garden soil, it will contain weed seeds, and possibly pests or disease, and it's unlikely to provide the perfect drainage and balanced nutrition that your edible crops need. You absolutely can make your own potting mix: you want to mix something that feeds plants (like compost), something that improves drainage (like sand, just make sure it's coarse builder's sand, or perlite) and something that holds water (like coconut coir or leaf mould). But you can buy excellent potting mixes too and frankly, if you are starting out or only have a few pots, that's what I would do.

With potting mix, you get what you pay for. A good one should feel light, almost fluffy. That's a sign of good porosity, as in there are spaces – which are called pores – between the particles of soil. Those spaces hold the water and air that your vege crops (and indeed soil life) need, and they allow a plant's roots to push easily through the soil. Don't buy potting mix that feels compacted in the bag, and never buy a bag that's gotten wet – it makes a mess of your car, for one thing, but also if the mix gets soaked in the bag, it will compact, and also if the fertiliser in the mix comes in contact with water it can start to be released.

Look for a potting mix that contains a controlled-release fertiliser, which will be released gradually over time; plus one that contains water storage crystals, which absorb many times their weight in water and hold it so it doesn't just run through the pot and trickle out the bottom; or a wetting agent, which helps with water penetration and retention.

You can buy bags of specialty tomato mix, potato mix, herb mix, citrus mix, fruit mix and strawberry mix. But frankly, you don't have to. They are always more expensive, and the main difference is usually just the fertiliser, as in the tomato mix will contain more potassium to encourage flower set and fruit; the herb mix will contain more nitrogen, which promotes leafy growth. I use a good general potting mix for everything I grow in containers, and then the right fertiliser for whatever I am growing.

If you are opening and handling bagged potting mixes or compost, wear a mask and gloves, work in a ventilated space and open the bag slowly with scissors rather than ripping it open. Wash your hands thoroughly after working with soil. There's a small chance that bagged soil mixes can contain a harmful microorganism that can cause Legionnaires' disease. I used to be a bit cavalier about this – the risk is very low, it's fair to say – but a few years ago I interviewed a gardener who had been affected by Legionnaires' disease, and it sounded horrible, so I am much more sensible and cautious now.

How to water pots

Watering is the make-or-break factor when it comes to success growing in pots. A good potting mix, as mentioned, should contain water storage crystals, which remain effective for about five years (after which they biodegrade) or a wetting agent, which usually remains effective for just a few months. These are both useful and help reduce the frequency of watering required, but you need to be prepared to water, and water often, probably every day, and in small pots or at the height of summer, it might be twice a day.

I try and water pots in the morning. If I forget I water in the evening but that means there's lots of water present at night, which slugs and snails love. You often see it said not to water in the middle of the day, which is because it wastes a lot of the water as it evaporates or is wicked away by wind before the plant can take it up. But if a plant in a pot is wilting and clearly stressed by a lack of water, water it immediately whatever the time is.

Apply water to pots slowly and at soil level. If you try and water quickly – as a water-blasting jet rather than a gentle trickle – you apply water faster than the soil can absorb it and usually wash some of your expensive potting mix right out of the pots. Over time too it affects your soil structure as any tiny particles of soil or dust get washed along and fill those pores that you want to have between soil particles.

But overwatering causes nearly as many problems as underwatering. If you are not sure, stick your finger into the soil. If the potting mix is dry on top but damp below, you might not need to water depending on the crop. And don't leave veges growing in pots sitting in water. Yes, plants roots need water but they also need oxygen. If the water in the soil cannot drain away then those pores between the soil particles, where oxygen should be, are full of water and the plants will eventually suffocate and die. You can and should mulch plants in pots. It will reduce water loss, feed soil and improve soil structure, and prevent weeds from germinating. Just ensure that the soil in the pot is moist before you put the mulch down, otherwise it keeps moisture out of the soil just as effectively as it keeps moisture in.

If you are growing fruiting plants in pots, like tomatoes or chillies, try deliberately putting them under slight drought stress, by which I mean giving them about 80 percent of the water you think they need, after the fruit has set and is ripening. That water stress will mean the plants produce more of the antioxidant compounds and flavour volatiles: so, tomatoes will be more flavoursome, and chillies will be hotter. You can do that with plants in the garden too, it's just much easier to control in pots.

Some crops need more water than others. Leafy green salad leaves, say, need the soil in which they are growing to stay constantly moist: they bolt if they dry out and because they are shallow-rooted, the roots are up in the top layer of soil, which dries out first. Whereas I find root crops and Mediterranean herbs can cope with the soil in a pot drying out before I water it again. If you are growing a few things in pots, group them according to their watering requirements: that way you can check on the ones that need daily checks more easily.

Feeding edibles in pots

A good potting mix contains a controlled-release fertiliser but the plants you grow will take the nutrients in it and use them up over a few months. I try to water edible crops in pots with a suitable liquid fertiliser every fortnight or so while they are actively growing. You can use granular controlled-release fertilisers in pots, or spikes or prills, but I find liquid fertilisers are a bit gentler. I also use them at half-strength or even quarter-strength. *NZ Gardener's* houseplant columnist Anna Gervai taught me the weakly-weekly approach to feeding houseplants (apply fertiliser at a higher dilution but more often, it doesn't have to be weekly per se, just regularly) and I now do that with my edibles too, especially in pots. It's cheaper and it reduces the risk of over-fertilising. I add compost to the soil in pots too, as the original potting mix settles, and bacterial action breaks the nutrients in the compost down over time to feed the plants. Never fertilise plants that are clearly under stress, such as wilting from drought. You might want to lavish them with attention after neglecting them, but if a plant's systems are not working well then feeding them simply adds more stress to their lives. Wait until they have fully recovered before applying fertiliser, and I would use a liquid fertiliser at a quarter strength at first.

You do not need to add any extra fertiliser, or other soil amendments like gypsum or compost, to a decent bought potting mix at the time of planting, and in fact, it can be actively unhelpful to do so. A good mix should already contain everything the plants need in a very carefully considered ratio and if you add ingredients it's likely to upset that ratio in a way that is detrimental to the performance of your plants.

Top crops for pots

Dwarf beans

A few years ago, I called a few horticultural experts and asked for their favourite dwarf bean. They almost universally selected the astonishingly prolific 'Top Crop' and that's the one I grow every year now. I reckon dwarf (aka bush) beans are much easier in pots than climbing (aka runner) beans although dwarf beans are determinate, which means they produce all their flowers – and therefore all the beans – in one big go. Climbing beans keep producing beans, so are more prolific: but they need a lot of water to fruit well. It's absolutely possible to grow them in pots, I know lots of gardeners who do so, just go for a bigger pot and keep the water up.

Broad beans

You can grow broad beans in pots too but go for a dwarf variety, like 'Dwarf Early Green', which doesn't need to be staked.

Capsicums

You can grow pretty much any capsicum in a big pot, although they take a while. Look out for what are often called snack peppers, like 'Dwarf Snack Red', 'Dwarf Snack Yellow' and 'Dwarf Snack Orange', they produce little fruit not much longer than my longest finger which you can eat raw. They are great for vege crudites, snacks and kids' lunchboxes. 'Candy Cane' even starts out with green-striped fruit, although they do, disappointingly, ripen to plain red.

Chillies

Any old chilli will do OK in a decent-sized pot plus growing them in pots means, when the chilli season is over, you can overwinter them (which means keeping them going to plant again next year). This gives you a head start on the growing season in year two, so your chillies should be fruiting sooner and for longer than the ones newly planted that year. If you want to overwinter a plant in a pot, at the end of the season just harvest any remaining fruit and trim the plants back, then move the whole plant into a warmish space, like a tunnelhouse, sunny potting shed or conservatory or even inside your house. Chillies won't keep growing or producing over winter – don't water them much, they don't need it – but when it is warm enough to plant chillies outside again, shift them back out and they should be up and away.

Zucchinis

Zucchini plants sprawl all over the place in the vegetable garden but keeping them in pots keeps their size in check. It also reduces the yield, but with zucchinis that's no bad thing. Just go for one zucchini in a big pot: no smaller than 30L.

Clockwise from top left: Some edibles look so pretty in pots you can grow them as ornamentals; a bean in a hanging basket; a productive chilli; a zucchini.

Clockwise from top left: Microgreens; herbs; a cucumber; lettuce and leafy greens.

Cucumber

You can grow most cucumbers in big pots but if you only have a small garden try the cucumber 'Spacemaster'. The cucumbers are little, the same size you'd pickle a gherkin at, but you can use them as salad cucumbers. The plant has a very compact, bushy habit, it only takes up about a third as much space as a standard cucumber. 'Iznik Mini' or 'Patio Snacker' are also great for pots and small gardens. Remember, cucumber can be grown as climbing plants too: growing one up an obelisk or a tipi in a pot gives you a lot of return for the space it takes up. Just regularly tie the vine onto the support with something soft and stretchy.

Eggplants

I find eggplant seedlings pretty hit and miss on their own roots even when growing them in my main garden so if you want to grow eggplants in the more stressful growing environment of a pot, seriously, don't be a hero: just go for a grafted eggplant. They cost more, yes, but they are so much easier, faster and more productive. You can often find the small-fruiting 'Ophelia', which produces cute little purple eggplants about 10cm long, as a grafted plant; that's a great choice for pots as it's quicker to fruit. But baba ghanoush is right up there with air, water and Netflix in my hierarchy of basic needs so I have grown the larger-fruited 'Bengun' as a grafted plant in pots too and got a good harvest from that, although it probably takes a whole month longer.

Herbs

You can grow almost any herb in a pot, and I grow loads in pots at home. I find, with Mediterranean herbs especially, pots give them the perfect drainage they prefer: indeed, I have had much better luck with sage in a pot than I have done with sage in the ground. But I also grow basil, bay, parsley (Italian and curly), chives, thyme, tarragon, rosemary, mint, oregano, coriander and several types of mint in pots too, just so I can have them right by the kitchen door for ease of harvesting.

Lettuces and leafy greens

All leafy salad-y things are great in pots, just keep on top of the irrigation or go for a self-watering planter. Go for non-hearting or cut-and-come-again types so you can pick individual leaves rather than harvest whole plants. Asian greens, like bok choy, tatsoi and wong bok, are all lovely in salads when the leaves are young, and fast and foolproof in pots. So if you have trouble with lettuces give them a grow instead.

Microgreens

You barely need instructions for microgreens, just scatter seeds thickly on top of soil, water and start snipping as soon as the true leaves appear. You can grow them in pretty much anything, but I think a seed-raising tray, or something wide and shallow like that, is best as it gives you a lot of surface area.

Potatoes

You can grow potatoes in pots, and I do. The yield is probably half what I'd get if I grew them in the ground, but they are still absolutely delicious. You could give main-crop potatoes a go, but frankly I find the faster-growing earlies like 'Rocket' and 'Swift' are your best bet for pots: and main-crop spuds don't do so well for me (probably because they take longer to produce and so are still growing as the weather gets hot, soil in a pot warms up pretty quickly anyway and potatoes prefer a cool root run). You can put one seed potato in a container the size of a bucket, or around three in a 50L tub.

Radishes, carrots and beetroot

Radishes are pretty much small enough to grow in any container, but some varieties of carrot and beetroot need more soil depth so go for a pot or a container that's at least 30cm deep. Or go for the cute little round carrot varieties, such as 'Paris Market' or 'Rolly Polly', and miniature beetroot varieties like 'Bonny Baby' or 'Baby Beets'. Or grow any other beetroot variety actually, just treat it as a baby beetroot and harvest it when it is small.

Spinach, silverbeet, kale and spring onions

These will all do brilliantly in a container; pick the leaves as required.

Tomatoes

Tomatoes can do brilliantly in pots, but stick to determinate or bush tomatoes, especially the ones that have been bred to suit container life such as 'Tumbling Tom Red' and 'Tumbling Tom Yellow'. 'Container Choice Red F1' is great in pots, it produces decent-sized fruit (about 150–200g each) on a nice compact plant that never gets much more than 60cm tall; 'Balcony F1' gets to about 60cm high too but the fruit are cherry tom-sized. 'Siderno' is another tomato bred for pots and small urban gardens, it never gets much taller than 45cm and produces masses of golf-ball-sized cherry tomatoes. Or try cherry 'Golden Cascade' in a hanging basket, the short stems get so heavy with fruit, they hang down over the sides.

You can actually grow tall tomatoes in pots too, although they need support. I like the Tomtwist stakes, where you just clip the stem onto the stake with little bread-bag clip-like clips. Paul Wylaars from Zealandia Horticulture Ltd told me when his dad was in a rest home, he bought him a Tomato Grow Tower from Tui, which is a self-watering pot with an attached extendable support tower or tomato cage. Zealandia sell a double-grafted cherry tomato which has a red variety and a yellow variety grafted onto the same plant, so his dad planted one of those and when the plant reached 1.5m (which is the height of the available support) he nipped out the growing tip, so the plant put its energy into the fruit. "It was a great way for him to have something growing on his deck, and very productive," Paul says.

Clockwise from top left: Tomatoes can be grown in hanging baskets, but get the variety right; potatoes in pots; I often grow spuds in grow bags; spring onions.

Useful charts

Let the soil temperature be your guide as to when to sow seed, give everything enough room and interplant fast- and slow-maturing crops.

Sowing chart

Temperature range for optimal germination

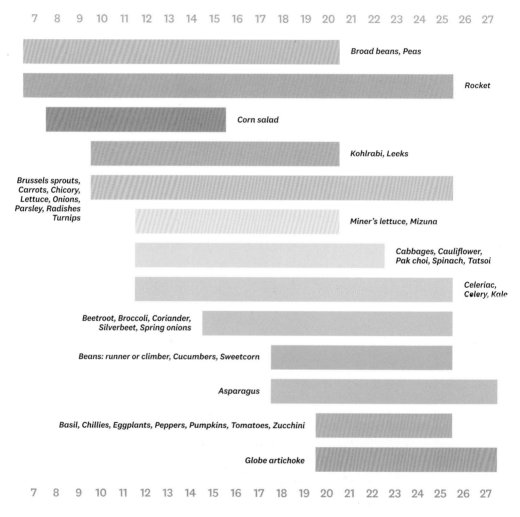

7 8 9 10 11 12 13 14 15 16 17 18 19 20 21 22 23 24 25 26 27

Broad beans, Peas

Rocket

Corn salad

Kohlrabi, Leeks

Brussels sprouts, Carrots, Chicory, Lettuce, Onions, Parsley, Radishes Turnips

Miner's lettuce, Mizuna

Cabbages, Cauliflower, Pak choi, Spinach, Tatsoi

Celeriac, Celery, Kale

Beetroot, Broccoli, Coriander, Silverbeet, Spring onions

Beans: runner or climber, Cucumbers, Sweetcorn

Asparagus

Basil, Chillies, Eggplants, Peppers, Pumpkins, Tomatoes, Zucchini

Globe artichoke

7 8 9 10 11 12 13 14 15 16 17 18 19 20 21 22 23 24 25 26 27

Degrees Celsius

You'll never regret the money you spend on a soil thermometer; it lets you time when to sow your vegetable crops far more precisely. Measure soil temperature in the morning, when the soil is at its coolest not after it has warmed up in the sun. Take a reading three or four days in a row and use the average: one reading is not really enough. These temperatures are the suggested range for optimal germination: seed might still germinate at higher and lower temperatures, just not as well.

Germination chart

How many days does it take to strike?

| 4 | 5 | 6 | 7 | 8 | 9 | 10 | 11 | 12 | 13 | 14 | 15 | 16 | 17 | 18 | 19 | 20 | 21 | 22 | 23 | 24 | 25 | 26 | 27 | 28 | 29 | 30 |

Radishes

Cauliflower

Lettuce

Kohlrabi

Zucchini

Miner's lettuce, Mizuna

Broad beans, Cabbages, Cucumbers, Kale, Peas, Tatsoi

Beans: dwarf or bush, Broccoli, Brussels sprouts, Coriander, Corn salad, Pak choi, Rocket, Spinach, Turnips

Celery, Eggplants, Pumpkins, Tomatoes

Chillies

Peppers

Basil, Beans: runner or climber, Chicory, Globe artichoke

Spring onions, Sweetcorn

Beetroot, Leeks, Silverbeet

Carrots

Onions

Parsley

Celeriac

Asparagus

| 4 | 5 | 6 | 7 | 8 | 9 | 10 | 11 | 12 | 13 | 14 | 15 | 16 | 17 | 18 | 19 | 20 | 21 | 22 | 23 | 24 | 25 | 26 | 27 | 28 | 29 | 30 |

Days

Spacing chart

How far apart should you plant it?

Asparagus	25cm	Coriander	15-25cm	Peas	10-15cm
Basil	15-20cm	Corn salad	5-10cm	Peppers	30-45cm
Beans: climber/runner	10-20cm	Cucumbers	30-100cm	Potatoes	30-60cm
Beans: dwarf/bush	15-25cm	Eggplants	45-60cm	*Main-crop spuds need to be about twice as far apart as earlies*	
Beetroot	10-20cm	Garlic	10-20cm	Pumpkins	1-2m
Broad beans	15-25cm	Globe artichoke	100cm	Radishes	5-10cm
Broccoli	45-80cm	Kale	15-30cm	*Daikon, or Japanese radish, needs more space, leave about 15cm*	
Sprouting broccoli needs the most room		Kohlrabi	15-25cm	Rocket	5-10cm
Brussels sprouts	50-60cm	Kūmara	30-45cm	*Arugula, or wild rocket, needs to be about 15cm apart*	
Cabbages	35-75cm	Leeks	20-25cm	Silverbeet	30cm
Chinese cabbages can be 30-40cm apart		Lettuce	10-30cm	Spinach	10-20cm
Carrots	5-8cm	Miner's lettuce	5cm	Spring onions	5-10cm
Cauliflower	30-60cm	Mizuna	10-40cm	Sweetcorn	30-50cm
Celeriac	30-75cm	*Space at 10cm if growing cut-and-come-again for salad leaves*		Tatsoi	20cm
Celery	60cm	Onions	10-15cm	Tomatoes	30-75cm
Chicory/radicchio	20-30cm	Pak choi	10-25cm	Turnip	5-15cm
Chillies	45-60cm	Parsley	15-30cm	Zucchini	100cm

To be honest, you should treat these two charts as fairly flexible guidelines rather than iron-fast rules. Different varieties of the same vegetable can have different spacing requirements and there are compact varieties of many of the vegetables in this list that don't need as much room. Plus, you can get away with planting closer if you are harvesting earlier – eating beetroot as baby beets say, rather than fully grown. The time to harvest is also affected by all sorts of variables in terms of the growing conditions; plus, you can harvest some things sooner but smaller – like leafy crops at the baby leaf stage. Also, when I am talking about time to harvest, sometimes it's time from planting (as in planting a seedling that I have grown or bought) and sometimes I am talking about the time from direct sowing. That just reflects how I grow those particular crops, but be aware you might need to adjust your expectations if you start from seed something I plant as a seedling.

Harvesting chart

How long does it take to grow?

Asparagus	two years from transplant	**Leeks**	120 days from direct sowing
Basil	60-70 days from transplant	**Lettuce**	50-60 days from planting
Beans: climber/runner	80 days from direct sowing	**Miner's lettuce**	45 days from direct sowing
Beans: dwarf/bush	60 days from direct sowing	**Mizuna**	30 days from direct sowing
Beetroot	55 days from direct sowing	**Mustard greens**	25-45 days from direct sowing
Broad beans	75 days from direct sowing	**Onions**	120 days from direct sowing
Broccoli	80-90 days from planting	**Pak choi**	40-60 days from planting

Sprouting broccoli is usually slower

		Parsley	60-80 days from direct sowing
Brussels sprouts	120 days from planting	**Peas**	55-65 days from direct sowing
Cabbages	50-100 days from planting	**Peppers**	80 days from planting
		Potatoes	70-150 days from planting

'Savoy' cabbage is the slowest

Carrots	70-75 days from direct sowing		*Main-crop spuds take about twice as long as earlies*
Cauliflower	45-90 days from planting	**Pumpkins**	100-150 days from planting
Celeriac	90 days from planting	**Radishes**	30 days from direct sowing
Celery	80-90 days from planting		

Daikon, or Japanese radish, take about 55 days from direct sowing

Chicory/radicchio	75 days from transplant	**Rocket**	30 days from direct sowing

Arugula, or wild rocket, takes about 50 days from direct sowing

Chillies	80 days from planting		
Coriander	40-65 days from direct sowing	**Silverbeet**	55-65 days from direct sowing
Corn salad	60 days from direct sowing	**Spinach**	40-45 days from direct sowing
Cucumbers	50-65 days from planting	**Spring onions**	70-90 days from direct sowing
Eggplants	60-90 days from planting	**Sweetcorn**	90-100 days from direct sowing
Garlic	5-7 months from planting	**Tatsoi**	45 days from direct sowing
Globe artichoke	20-28 weeks from planting	**Tomatoes**	60-85 days from transplant
Kale	50-75 days from direct sowing	**Turnip**	50 days from direct sowing
Kohlrabi	60 days from direct sowing	**Zucchini**	55 days from transplant
Kūmara	100-120 days from planting slips		

Shout-outs

I am grateful to a lot of people who have helped me create this book. First, to the designer Olivia Tuck, who is very much the co-creator of *Vege Patch from Scratch* and who made it look much better than I could have imagined. Thank you so much Olivia, for the talent, time and mahi you have contributed. Thanks too to my good friends: the photographer Sally Tagg, who took so many of the beautiful images on these pages; and the copy editor Síana Clifford (especially for the deadline doughnuts). I am also grateful to Alison Brook from Upstart Press for suggesting I write this book in the first place.

I was lucky that so many knowledgeable gardeners from across New Zealand shared their expertise with me so generously. In particular, I would like to thank Jack Hobbs, Jodi Roebuck, Yotam and Niva Kay, Dr Nick Roskruge (Ātiawa and Ngāti Tama), Jane Wrigglesworth, Carl Freeman, Candy Harris, Scott Bromwich, Adrian Sutherland (Ngāti Porou), Gary Patterson, Dr Jessica Hutchings (Ngāi Tahu, Ngāti Huirapa, Gujarati), Paul Wylaars, Renee Davies, and Bart Acres. Thanks also to the whole team at *NZ Gardener*, Mei Leng Wong, Sarah Scully and William Hansby, who have all helped out with this project and kept me sane along the way.

And finally, to my family: my thanks to my parents Hugh and Rosaleen for all the support you show me, always; to my two lovely sisters Jane and Kate; and to Conrad and Dusty for being there through the whole thing.

And I am grateful to whoever is reading this too. I hope there's something in the pages of this book that inspires you to get growing. And I hope your garden flourishes and brings you joy.

Good Books

I have a big collection of gardening books and consult them frequently. These are a few of my favourites.

The Abundant Garden by Niva & Yotam Kay
The Edible Backyard by Kath Irvine
The Cook's Herb Garden and *The Cook's Salad Garden*, both by Mary Browne, Helen Leach & Nancy Tichborne
Garden Pest & Disease Control: Essential NZ Guide and *The Home Orchard: Essential NZ Guide to Fruit Growing*, both by Bill Brett
The Salad Garden by Joy Larkcom
How to Grow More Vegetables by John Jeavons
One Magic Square by Lolo Houbein
Koanga Garden Guide by Kay Baxter
The Everyday Herbalist by Jane Wrigglesworth
Grow it Yourself Vegetables by Andrew Steens
An Illustrated Guide to Common Weeds of New Zealand by Ian Popay, Paul Champion & Trevor James
The New Zealand Organic Gardening Handbook by Brenda Little
The New Zealand Vegetable Garden by Jonathan Spade
Vegetable Growing in New Zealand by J.A. McPherson & F.J.E. Jollie
Organic Vegetable Gardening by Annette McFarlane

_____

And of course, I consult old copies of *NZ Gardener* all the time. The contributors include the very best and most knowledgeable horticulturists and plantspeople in New Zealand. I'm not biased at all, just stating facts.

MATTHEWS ON GARDENING — L. W. MATTHEWS AND BARBARA MATTHEWS — Reed

GROWING TOMATOES — Everything You Need to Know Explained Simply — Including Heirloom Tomatoes

the salad garden — joy larkcom

Organic Vegetable Gardening — Annette McFarlane — ABC

Yates GARDEN GUIDE — Collins

GARDEN PEST & DISEASE CONTROL — ESSENTIAL NZ GUIDE — BILL BRETT — BOOKS

The Organic Guide to Edible Gardens — Jennifer Stackhouse & Debbie McDonald

herb garden — Browne, Leach & Tichborne — cpp

the cook's ... revisited

JEAVONS — HOW TO GROW MORE VEGETABLES

The Abundant Garden — Niva & Yotam K...

ANDREW STEENS — GROW IT YOURSELF VEGETABLES — Bateman

The Everyday Herbalist — Jane Wrigglesworth — A&U

THE HOME ORCHARD — ESSENTIAL NZ GUIDE TO GROWING FRUIT — BILL BRETT

THE NEW ZEALAND Organic Gardening Handbook — Brenda Little

THE EDIBLE BACKYARD — KATH IRVINE — Godwit

One Magic Square — Lolo Houbein

Index

Page numbers in green refer to the main entries for each heading

Index

Page numbers in green refer to the main entries for each heading

From Jo's garden.
Gerkins, page 163;
tomato salsa, page 152.

Credits

All images are from Adobe Stock except those below

Cover, Title, Contents, Author's Letter
Sally Tagg

Garden illustrations
Renee Davies

Chapter 1: How to get growing
Sally Tagg, Adrian Sutherland
(@OneMinuteGardening), Rachel Clare,
Diana Maunder, Dawn Ballagh

Chapter 2: Soil is everything
Sally Tagg, Rose Hughes, Candy Harris
(@nzgardener), Paul McCredie,
Kath Irvine (@edible.backyard)

Chapter 3: Grow more plants
Sally Tagg, GAP Photos, Paul McCredie

Chapter 4: 365 days of salad
Sally Tagg, Candy Harris (@nzgardener),
Julique (Aus), Sophie Thomson (Aus),
Auckland Botanic Gardens, Sheryn Dean,
Ezra Alexander (@DIYplantman)

Chapter 5: Grow herbs everywhere
Sally Tagg, GAP Photos/Friedrich Strauss

Chapter 6: Spring is here
Sally Tagg, Rachel Clare, Jamie Tucker
(@LaughingPukekoOrganics)

Chapter 7: Summer at last
Sally Tagg, Paul McCredie,
Candy Harris (@nzgardener),
Claire Mossong

Chapter 8: Autumn harvests
Sally Tagg, GAP Photos, Juliet Nicholas,
Candy Harris (@nzgardener),
Claire Mossong, Fiona Tomlinson,
Bart Acres (@mycologic.nz),
Robert Guyton

Chapter 9: Winter is coming
Sally Tagg

Chapter 10: Small spaces
Sally Tagg, Amanda Clark(@mykiwilife),
Caitlin Huynh (@my_concrete_garden),
Vegepod, Belinda Stone, Caitlin Te Tai
(@yourgreenthumbpal), Lisa Robinson

Chapter 11: Pots & containers
Sally Tagg, GAP Photos/Friedrich Strauss,
GAP Photos/Nicola Stocken

Chapter 12: Useful charts
Sally Tagg

Shout-outs & Good Books
Sally Tagg

Jo McCarroll's
Vege Patch
from scratch

A catalogue record for this book is available
from the National Library of New Zealand

ISBN 978-1-77694-016-5

An Upstart Press Book
Published in 2023 by Upstart Press Ltd.
26 Greenpark Road, Penrose,
Auckland 1061. New Zealand

 upstart press

Text © Jo McCarroll 2023
Design and Format © Upstart Press 2023
The moral rights of the author have been asserted.

All rights reserved. No part of this publication may be reproduced
or transmitted in any form or by any means, electronic or mechanical,
including photocopying, recording, or any information storage and
retrieval system, without permission in writing from the publisher.

Senior commissioning editor: Alison Brook
Design and Art Direction: Olivia Tuck
Photographer: Sally Tagg
Garden Design: Renee Davies

Printed by Everbest Printing Co. Ltd, China
on paper sourced from sustainable forests.